The Second Wo
War Explained

The Second World War Explained

Michael O'Kelly

Pen & Sword
MILITARY

First published in Great Britain in 2018 by
Pen & Sword Military
An imprint of
Pen & Sword Books Ltd
47 Church Street
Barnsley
South Yorkshire
S70 2AS

ISBN 978 1 52673 743 4

A CIP catalogue record for this book is
available from the British Library.

Printed and bound in England by TJ International Ltd, Padstow, Cornwall

Pen & Sword Books Limited incorporates the imprints of Atlas, Archaeology,
Aviation, Discovery, Family History, Fiction, History, Maritime, Military, Military
Classics, Politics, Select, Transport, True Crime, Air World, Frontline Publishing,
Leo Cooper, Remember When, Seaforth Publishing, The Praetorian Press,
Wharncliffe Local History, Wharncliffe Transport, Wharncliffe True Crime and
White Owl.

For a complete list of Pen & Sword titles please contact
PEN & SWORD BOOKS LIMITED
47 Church Street, Barnsley, South Yorkshire, S70 2AS, England
E-mail: enquiries@pen-and-sword.co.uk
Website: www.pen-and-sword.co.uk

Contents

Maps   vii

Preface   xvii

Chapter 1   Background to War   1

Chapter 2   September 1939 to June 1940   5

Chapter 3   The Battle of Britain: Summer 1940   21

Chapter 4   The Blitz and Wartime Great Britain   25

Chapter 5   The Mediterranean Theatre 1941 and 1942   31

Chapter 6   Battle of the Atlantic 1941 and 1942   39

Chapter 7   Germany Invades the Soviet Union   47

Chapter 8   Royal Navy Arctic Convoys 1941–45   57

Chapter 9   Japan Enters the War, December 1941 to June 1944   61

Chapter 10   The Holocaust   79

Chapter 11   UK Bomber Command   83

Chapter 12   Soviet Union 1942 and Stalingrad   89

Chapter 13   Malta, El Alamein and North Africa 1942–43   95

Chapter 14   The Battle of the Atlantic 1943: The Decisive Year   103

Chapter 15   Sicily and Italy 1943–44   107

Chapter 16   Soviet Union 1943 and 1944   115

Chapter 17   Invasion of France 1944   125

Chapter 18   The Far East 1944 and 1945   145

Chapter 19   Final Defeat of Germany 1945   161

Chapter 20   The Atom Bomb   177

Appendix 1   Meetings of Great Power Leaders   181

Appendix 2   Second World War Timeline   185

Index   193

Maps

Burma (now Myanmar)

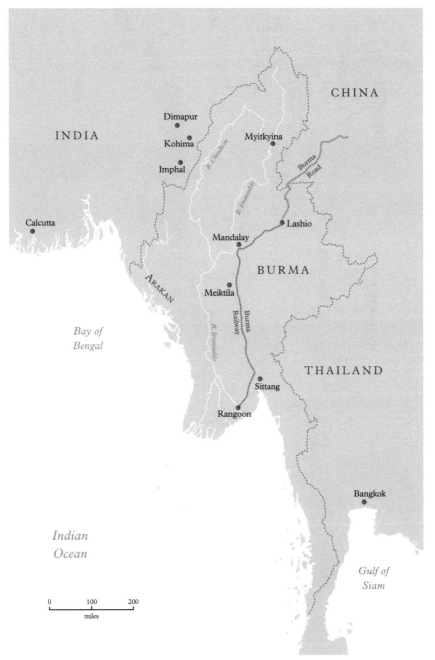

D-Day Landings

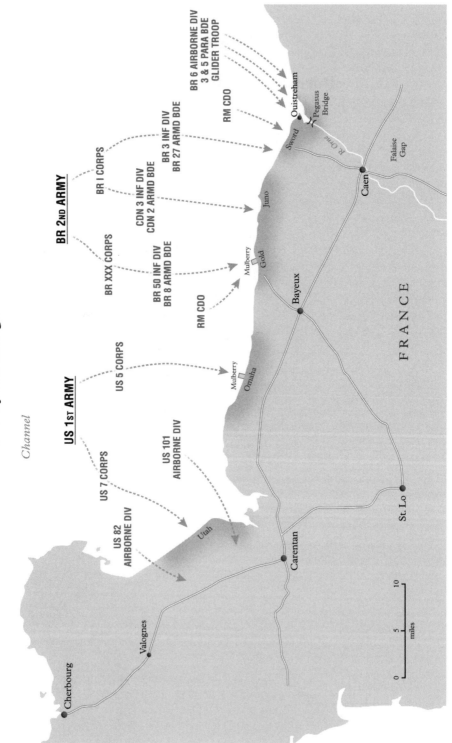

Channel

BR 2ND ARMY

BR 6 AIRBORNE DIV
3 & 5 PARA BDE
GLIDER TROOP

RM CDO

BR 3 INF DIV
BR 27 ARMD BDE

BR I CORPS

CDN 3 INF DIV
CDN 2 ARMD BDE

BR XXX CORPS

BR 50 INF DIV
BR 8 ARMD BDE

RM CDO

US 1ST ARMY

US 5 CORPS

US 7 CORPS

US 101
AIRBORNE DIV

US 82
AIRBORNE DIV

Ouistreham
Pegasus Bridge
Sword
R. Orne
Caen
Falaise Gap
Juno
Gold
Mulberry
Bayeux
Mulberry
Omaha
FRANCE
Utah
Carentan
St. Lo
Valognes
Cherbourg

0   5   10
miles

Eastern Europe

NORWAY

SWEDEN

DENMARK

FINLAND

Lake
Ladoga

Leningrad

Tallinn
ESTONIA

LATVIA

LITHUANIA

Königsberg
EAST
PRUSSIA

Danzig

R. Vistula

Hamburg

R. Elbe

Berlin

GERMANY

Breslau

Prague

CZECHOSLOVAKIA

R. Danube

SWITZERLAND

AUSTRIA

ITALY

POLAND

Warsaw

Minsk

BELORUSSIA

Smolensk

Pripet
Marshes

Budapest

HUNGARY

YUGOSLAVIA

Belgrade

ALBANIA

Moscow

Kursk

Kharkov

Kiev

UKRAINE

U.S.S.R.

R. Dnieper

R. Don

R. Volga

Stalingrad

Astrakhan

CAUCASUS

Crimean
Sea

CRIMEA
Yalta
Sevastopol

Black
Sea

ROMANIA

Bucharest

BULGARIA

GREECE

TURKEY

0   100   200
miles

Pacific War

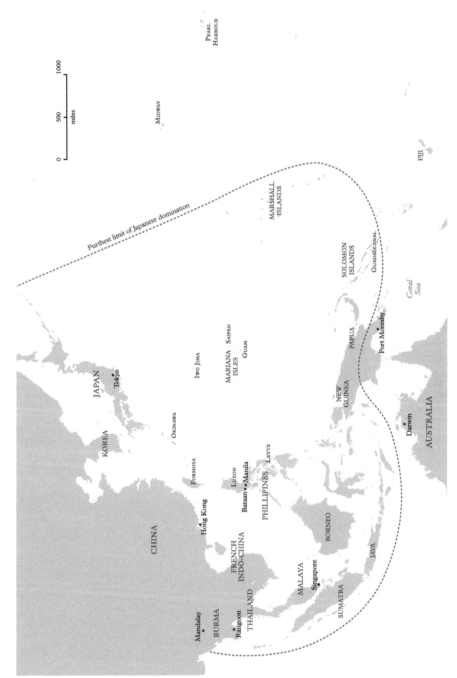

War in Italy

Mediterranean and Desert War

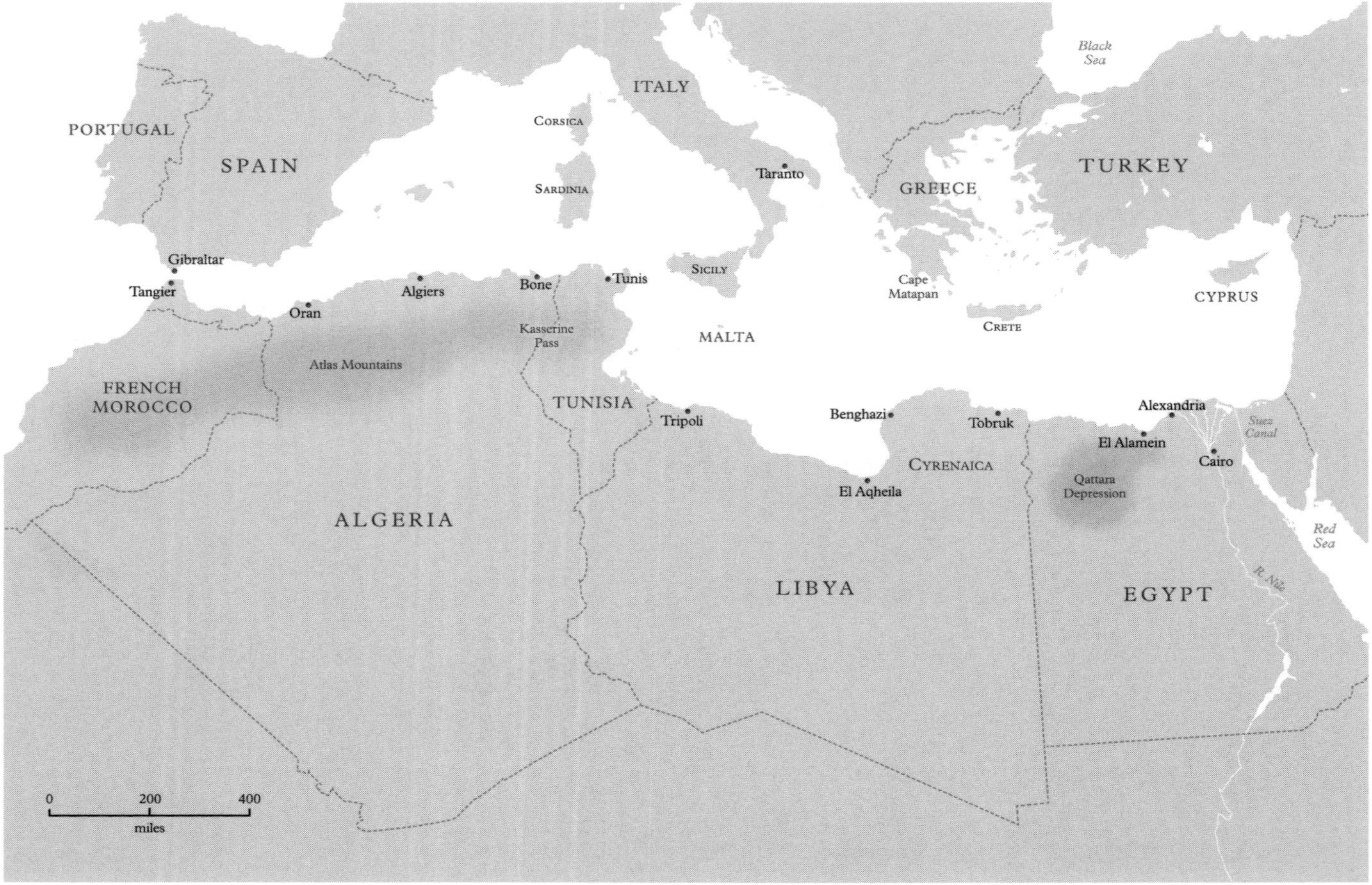

North Atlantic Convoy Routes

GREENLAND

ICELAND

CANADA

NEWFOUNDLAND

St John's

Sydney

Halifax

2,500 - 3,000 miles depending on route

Air
Gap

THE AZORES

FRANCE

R. Loire

St Nazaire

Lorient

Glasgow

Liverpool

SPAIN

Gibraltar

0   250   500

miles

Arctic Convoy Routes

GREENLAND

NOVAYA ZEMBLYA

SPITZBERGEN

BEAR ISLAND

Appoximate Summer Routes

Appoximate Winter Routes

ICELAND

Reykjavik

SCOTLAND

ORKNEYS

SHETLAND ISLANDS

NORWAY

Narvik

SWEDEN

FINLAND

Murmansk

Archangel

SOVIET UNION

0   100   200   300

miles

Western Front

Preface

Talking to some of my young friends I was surprised to find that this new generation seemed to know little or nothing about the Second World War. As that long and terrible conflict must be one of the most significant events in the whole history of the world, this seemed a pity. Some knowledge of the past may also help prevent a repetition that, with nuclear weapons, could end civilisation.

Of course many distinguished historians have written major histories of the conflict, but maybe their length and detail deter some people. Perhaps, I thought, a short account giving a rough idea of what happened might help to fill the gap. And perhaps it might inspire some to read one of those excellent full histories. It is only these that can convey an understanding of the true awfulness of the war and the appalling suffering it inflicted on millions.

There is nothing new or original in this book. It just contains material gleaned from the works of proper historians, plus a little from my imperfect memory. I fear there must be some mistakes but trust they will not falsify the general picture. Many statistics have had to be included to give some idea of scale. I hope there are no 'damned lies', but they are best taken as approximations.

I have had to make difficult decisions between confining a complex campaign to a short summary or including more detail because of my opinion of its importance or interest. Inevitably, many big battles are omitted. That others may disagree with the balance is understood, and they may well be right.

It is intended that profit from this work should benefit Armed Services charities. Meanwhile I should like to record great thanks to my sons for their helpful comments on various drafts, particularly Tim, who has been a tower of strength, and also to my ever patient editor Linne Matthews for her immensely valuable help.

Chapter 1

Background to War

By the end of the nineteenth century, Germany had been led by Chancellor Bismarck to become a mighty force dominating Europe. It had a large and successful army and enjoyed the close support of the Austro-Hungarian Empire. Kaiser William, Germany's emperor, was a grandson of Queen Victoria, whom he revered, and a nephew of the King of England, Edward VII. Germany and Great Britain were good friends, albeit under strain in the Boer War and as competitors when Admiral Tirpitz started to develop a rival battleship fleet.

Then came the enormous disaster of the First World War, in which Germany was defeated by the British Empire, France and the United States. In the 1920s, Germany was a broken country, financially ruined, hungry, and with huge unemployment. The German people were bitterly resentful of their defeat and the harsh terms imposed on their country by the Versailles Treaty.

Then a saviour appeared, or so they thought. In 1921, Adolf Hitler became leader of the National Socialist or Nazi Party, dedicated to the rebirth of a great Germany. His autobiography, *Mein Kampf*, published in the 1920s, set out his ghastly philosophy. Here he announced his hatred of what he believed were the world's two great evils: Communism and Judaism. He also emphasised that the Germans needed Lebensraum ('living space') and openly wrote of the future German expansion in the east. His later invasions of Czechoslovakia, Poland and the Soviet Union followed this claimed need. He believed Germans were a master race and was contemptuous of other nations.

Thus it is even more astonishing that Hitler and Soviet Union leader Joseph Stalin, in apparent friendship, signed a non-aggression pact in August 1939. This pact meant that the Soviet Union, as an ally of Nazi Germany, became a potential enemy of Britain. This position was of course then reversed by Hitler's invasion of Russia in 1941.

Hitler was clever, utterly ruthless, and stubbornly determined. He was a compelling orator who fired up the masses with his vision. He was also a leader who inspired huge loyalty in his close compatriots. One of his remarkable attributes was a quite phenomenal memory. He retained an encyclopaedic knowledge of the weaponry of other nations' ships, tanks and aircraft. His greatest flaw was in his often misguided strategic decision making, ignoring the advice of his military leaders.

Initially supported by the right-wing old guard of German politics as well as the army, Hitler's political manoeuvring eventually outwitted them both. While his thugs intimidated the opposition, the masses flocked to his support. Eventually, in 1933, Hitler was appointed Chancellor, akin to a prime minister. He quickly set about law-making to transform what had been a democracy into a dictatorship. He was supported by his own personal bodyguard, the SS (SchutzStaffel), which subsequently developed into an elite army, the Waffen-SS. When he became president as well as chancellor, he required all the armed forces to take an oath of personal allegiance to 'their Führer'. All moral considerations, all justice and all freedom were subordinated to the 'greater good of Germany'. Informers were encouraged by the dreaded secret police, the Gestapo, to report any opposition. Those considered by the Nazis to be 'enemies of society' were imprisoned or executed. Many thousands of mentally or physically disabled men, women and children were considered useless and were secretly killed by the SS. The Jews, unfairly held responsible for many of Germany's ills, were outlawed, ruthlessly persecuted and encouraged to flee the country.

Almost all children in Germany eventually became members of the Hitler Youth while all other youth organisations were banned. Thus Hitler created an enormous reservoir of young people who were brainwashed as Nazi warriors, happy to die for the Führer.

Hitler also introduced conscription and started a major rearmament programme designed to treble the size of the army in defiance of the Versailles Treaty. In his first five years in power he then successively gobbled up the Rhineland and Austria, and threatened Czechoslovakia. In 1938, with war seeming imminent, Neville Chamberlain, the British Prime Minister, paid three visits to Hitler, while the rest of the world voiced their ineffectual disapproval. Chamberlain was an honest and upright man, desperate to avoid or at least delay another terrible conflict only twenty years after the First World War had ended. Eventually, with the reluctant agreement of Czechoslovakia, it was accepted by France and Britain that Germany could occupy Sudetenland, the German-speaking section of that country. In return, Hitler gave a solemn pledge that he had no further territorial ambitions in Europe. Many rejoiced when Chamberlain returned home proclaiming the achievement of 'Peace in our time'.

However, it was less than a year before Hitler occupied the rest of Czechoslovakia and then later threatened to invade Poland. History has not been kind to Chamberlain. He is portrayed as being simple-minded and easily deceived in accepting the lies and broken promises of Adolf Hitler. But there is another view that suggests he was well aware of Hitler's duplicity and deceived the dictator into postponing the probably inevitable war. This gave Britain perhaps another year to increase the desperately needed rearmament long demanded by Churchill and others that he had put in train. Amongst many things it gave time to build the Hurricane and Spitfire fighter planes that won the Battle of Britain.

France and Britain tried to warn off Hitler from attacking Poland, but they had no success. In September 1939, Hitler commenced a savage invasion of that country, and so began the catastrophic Second World War. Five years later, between 50 and 60 million people had been killed, Germany destroyed and an exhausted Great Britain physically damaged and financially ruined.

Chapter 2

September 1939 to June 1940

Germany's strategic position was strengthened by the treaties of support they had made with Japan and Italy. The three powers became known as the Axis. Japan, who for nearly ten years had been fighting China, had a powerful army and navy but stayed out of the war for the first two years. Italy's fascist dictator, Benito Mussolini, was a particular friend and ally of Hitler. The United Kingdom was supported by the mighty British Empire. The armed forces of Canada, South Africa, India, Australia and New Zealand played a major role in the war.

Eire, although remaining neutral, denied the Royal Navy the use of Irish bases, which had initially been retained by Britain but were handed over as a goodwill gesture in 1938. These bases would have been of inestimable value in the Battle of the Atlantic. Sweden remained neutral but gave important assistance to Germany until near the end. Sweden then finally changed sides to support the winners. Switzerland stayed firmly neutral, as it had done in the First World War.

The UK and France were faced by a highly trained and well-equipped German Army of nearly 3 million men, called the Wehrmacht. Field Marshal Goering, Hitler's number two, controlled a large modern air force, the Luftwaffe. The navy was called the Kriegsmarine. Here the Germans had made a major strategic error in building big ships rather than the U-boats (submarines) that had proved so successful in the First World War. Their battleships were always a threat and forced Britain to develop major resources to counter them. But otherwise their achievements were small. In the Second World War, the U-boats, at first only a few in number, were an altogether greater threat, as we will see. Germany could easily have built many more. If they had, they might well have starved Britain of the supplies needed for survival and won the war.

For those unfamiliar with warship categories, the **battleship** was the heavily armoured biggest warship, with a main armament of large 15 or 16 inch calibre guns. It dominated the main navies of the world up until the Second World War. Its vulnerability to submarine attack, and even more to attack by aircraft, then became very evident. At the beginning of the war the major navies had few **aircraft carriers**. However, their important ability to launch aircraft attacks on ships hundreds of miles away was soon clearly understood. They became the building priority.

Destroyers were the small, fast workhorses, important in their anti-submarine role and also able to threaten large ships with torpedo attack. **Cruisers** may be seen as long-range ships, halfway in size and armament between the battleship and the destroyer. **Frigates** and **corvettes** were smaller and slower than destroyers, and designed primarily for anti-submarine operations.

The Germans also built four **'pocket' battleships** of reduced size, faster, but with smaller calibre (14 inch) guns. They had some limited success as commerce raiders.

The Royal Navy, together with the major navies of Japan and the United States, had also long relied on the power of big ships and big guns. The importance of aircraft at sea was not appreciated, nor the weak ability of the Royal Navy to counter the submarine threat. Radar equipment suitable for ships had still not yet been developed.

Radar is the well-known system that uses the reflection of radio waves to determine the range and direction of ships and aircraft, or indeed any solid object. It was being secretly developed by many nations in the years before the Second World War, with America and Britain leading the field. It had an important early use in detecting incoming enemy aircraft in the Battle of Britain. Later it became valuable in detecting enemy submarines on the surface. Now of course radar is a system with many uses and fitted to all ships and aircraft.

Britain's small regular army was only 224,000 strong, although conscription rapidly brought it up to one million. It lacked modern equipment and used out-of-date tactics. It took years to develop into the well-led effective fighting force of 2.9 million men that it eventually became.

As this book frequently mentions various types of army formations, it may be useful to summarise their approximate sizes, although these could vary greatly nation by nation and the circumstances of the time. The basic infantry unit able to operate semi-independently is the **battalion**, comprising three or four companies, totalling about 500 men. A **brigade**, containing a number of battalions, might then number 2,000 to 4,000. The **division** is normally a complete independent fighting formation including a number of supporting units such as artillery, anti-tank unit, signals, medical, engineers etc. Its size could vary greatly, normally from 10,000 to 18,000 soldiers. However, some German divisions in Russia in extremis were reduced to 2,000 men, and some Russian infantry divisions to 5,000. Two or more divisions might form a **corps**, and two or three of these bring you to an **army**, from 70,000 to 100,000 strong. Finally, two or three armies together make up an **army group**.

Britain's air force was small but expanding fast as modern aeroplanes such as the Spitfire and Hurricane came off the production line. However, Coastal Command was grievously neglected, having only comparatively short-range aircraft. It took years before US long-range Liberators showed how aircraft could be really effective in anti-submarine warfare. Bomber Command also lacked long-range aircraft.

France joined us in declaring war. They had a very large army but it lacked radio communication, and it was cumbersome and over reliant on its eastern fortification, the Maginot Line. France's air force had not been given enough priority and contained mostly obsolescent aircraft.

With the aid of the Soviet Union's army, Poland was quickly conquered, with unprecedented savagery. Over 500 towns and villages were burned to the ground. Hundreds of thousands of civilians, particularly Jews, were executed or deported to forced labour or concentration camps. Stalin ordered the arrest and execution of 22,000 prominent Polish leaders and military officers. France had threatened to help Poland by attacking Germany from the west, but in the end did nothing. Britain hurried an expeditionary force (BEF) of about ten divisions over to France, later increasing this to fifteen divisions. They were positioned in the north to defend against an attack through Belgium and Holland.

There was little or no land fighting in the first months of 1940, a period known as the 'phoney war'. But as the four-year-long Battle of the Atlantic started, the picture at sea was different. Great Britain relied for its existence on importing by sea most of its food, raw materials and oil. If German U-boats could sink enough ships to stop this flow, Great Britain would be defeated. The advantages of a convoy in which large groups of ships sailed in company, protected if possible by a screen of anti-submarine warships, were well known and put into practice. Luckily the German paucity of submarines at first kept our losses low. However, sinkings included HMS *Courageous*, one of the Royal Navy's five aircraft carriers, and then the battleship HMS *Royal Oak* was also torpedoed. The latter was in the Fleet anchorage Scapa Flow, in the Hebrides. This was thought to be impenetrable by submarines but the brave and skilful U-boat ace Günther Prien managed it. Both ships incurred very heavy loss of life.

One victory at sea, in December 1939, cheered the nation. It was called the Battle of the River Plate. The German pocket battleship

Graf Spee had sunk ten merchant ships in the Indian Ocean and South Atlantic when she unwisely attacked three light cruisers under Commodore Harwood who were looking for her outside Montevideo. She severely damaged HMS *Exeter*, but HMS *Ajax* and the New Zealand HMNZ *Achilles* were still fighting when *Graf Spee*, also damaged, broke off to enter neutral Montevideo to effect repairs. Then, deceived into believing a bigger Royal Navy force was arriving, her captain decided defeat was inevitable, and to avoid further loss of life he scuttled his ship in the harbour. *Ajax* and *Achilles*, who in fact had no support as yet, knew they were no match for the mighty *Graf Spee*, and were greatly relieved.

Graf Spee had a supply ship in company called *Altmark*, who disappeared from the scene with about 350 Merchant Navy prisoners arising from the pocket battleship's sinkings. When she was detected soon after in a neutral Norway fiord, Churchill gave instructions that she should be boarded by HMS *Cossack*, commanded by Captain (later Admiral) Vian. The sailors leapt aboard and opened the hold to effect the rescue, shouting, 'The navy's here.' It became a famous war cry.

The 'phoney war' ended in April 1940 when Hitler occupied Denmark. Simultaneously, a large German seaborne force invaded neutral Norway. Hitler was keen to safeguard the import of Scandinavian iron ore and also to protect the Baltic Sea. The UK had also decided to invade the north of Norway to deny Germany the precious iron ore, but Germany struck first. Battles raged by air, land and sea for two months. Our operations were badly planned, badly organised, and often characterised by order, counter order, and the enthusiastic but mistaken intervention of Winston Churchill, now the First Lord of the Admiralty. At one stage we captured Narvik, but finally withdrew early in June. The Norwegian Major Quisling sided with the Germans and announced himself as Prime Minister. The word 'quisling' entered the English language as a synonym for 'traitor'.

Perhaps one of many brave naval actions is of particular interest. Lieutenant Commander G.B. Roope commanding the destroyer *Glowworm* sought out and found the German heavy cruiser *Admiral Hipper*. He decided to attack and hopefully damage the *Hipper* before his small ship was destroyed in a completely unequal contest. Having missed with her torpedoes, *Glowworm* was heavily damaged as she approached and rammed the cruiser before herself capsizing and sinking. The extensive repairs needed to *Hipper* kept her out of action for much of the war. Roope was awarded a posthumous Victoria Cross (VC), the highest award for gallantry.

British naval forces suffered serious losses with the Luftwaffe demonstrating the importance of air superiority over the sea. German naval losses were greater, but this could not disguise the fact that a great naval power had suffered defeat in a major maritime campaign by a Continental land power with a small navy.

Britain's perceived operational incompetence and failure to stem the German invasion led in May to Prime Minister Neville Chamberlain being replaced by Winston Churchill, who somehow escaped blame for the Norway disaster. The country was thankfully now in the charge of a great orator and leader with immense experience, energy and determination. The outlook was transformed. Churchill formed a coalition government, with the Cabinet including representatives of all the major political parties. Like Hitler, Churchill had many unwise and mistaken strategic intentions, and was very difficult to work with. But unlike Hitler, in the end, albeit often after much sometimes angry argument, he accepted the decisions of the War Cabinet and his military advisers, the Chiefs of Staff. And again unlike Hitler, he didn't always sack those who disagreed with him. Wonderfully supported by his wife Clementine, without the drive and inspired leadership of this great man, it is difficult to see how Britain could have won the war.

The day Churchill assumed office, 10 May 1940, Hitler launched three armies totalling 136 divisions (including some 3,000 tanks) into France. The main thrust came unexpectedly through the Ardennes to Sedan. As in Poland, it used 'blitzkrieg' tactics, essentially a combination of concentration, speed and surprise. The Panzer Army was led by tanks on a narrow front combined with lorried infantry and supported by the Luftwaffe with its fearsome Stuka dive-bombers. Other German armies attacked France further south and also plunged into the Low Countries. The BEF and French armies advanced into Belgium to defend it. Elsewhere, the Germans, in fierce fighting, advanced with bewildering speed. The French Army outnumbered the Germans but was over reliant on the Maginot Line, which was quickly bypassed. Their command

and control was hopelessly disorganised. Reaction was slow and characterised by very poor communications and low morale. Movement was seriously hampered by hundreds of thousands of refugees clogging the roads. A week after defeating the French at Sedan, the Panzers reached the channel coast near Abbeville. The BEF and French armies in the north were now cut off. Supported by the RAF, who suffered heavy losses, these troops had fought valiantly but now could only fall back on Dunkirk. The Germans took many prisoners of war. In two incidents, a total of 185 of these unarmed British soldiers were massacred in cold blood by SS units. The latter also shot, after capture, something like 3,000 French colonial troop prisoners, mainly Senegalese, who had fought bravely in that terrible May.

At this moment the Axis offered negotiations to end Britain's part in the war. Faced with a decision of fundamental importance and great difficulty, the War Cabinet of six men spent long hours in agonising debate. Britain's ally France was effectively defeated and much of the British Army was expected to be destroyed at Dunkirk. Almost all Europe was conquered or allied with Germany. Was it reasonable to refuse the offer of negotiations and thus condemn many thousands of our young men to die in a war that we seemed certain to lose? And this only twenty-two years after the flower of the nation had been slaughtered on the battlefields of France?

Many serious and influential people believed we should negotiate an end. Their political leader was the much respected Foreign

Secretary Lord Halifax. He had only just refused the offer of the premiership for himself, and in Parliament and in the War Cabinet he had much support for his view. For many hours Churchill argued desperately against him. Eventually, fearing defeat, Churchill postponed any War Cabinet decision and called a meeting of the full twenty-five-member Cabinet. Here he set out his belief that 'negotiations' effectively meant some form of cowardly surrender to the forces of evil. With passionate oratory, which deeply moved his listeners, he proclaimed our duty to fight on, supported by the British Empire in a noble cause. His speech was received with cheers. It was a master stroke. When the War Cabinet resumed their meeting, all members including Halifax accepted that the debate was over and that Churchill had won the day. It is a chilling thought that Britain had so nearly dropped out of the conflict. Many think that in that event, Germany would probably have won the war. If alive at all, we should be living in a vassal state controlled under the evil doctrines of a Nazi empire.

But now back to the plight of the 400,000 soldiers at Dunkirk apparently facing destruction by the advancing Panzer armies. Astonishingly, General Von Rundstedt, wishing to conserve his exhausted forces for future battles in France, ordered a halt and was supported in this by Hitler. It seems to have been a crazy decision that allowed the brilliant Vice Admiral Ramsay time to arrange an evacuation of the BEF. He organised a huge armada of ferries, small ships and boats of all sizes – altogether nearly 900 craft – led by forty destroyers. Luckily the weather was calm. On the Dunkirk perimeter, French and British troops with great determination and fortitude kept large German forces at bay until the evacuation was complete. The RAF lost 149 aircraft but saved thousands of lives as they disrupted many of the constant German air attacks. Over nine days, some 338,000 men were brought back to the United Kingdom. About a third of them were French and a lesser number Polish. They left behind 65,000 vehicles, 20,000 motorcycles, 2,500 guns, over 400 tanks, and about 600,000 tons of stores. Six destroyers were lost to air attack, nineteen damaged, and over 200 smaller craft sunk or damaged. Altogether, the BEF lost 68,000 men killed, wounded, or captured. Britain would have been left defenceless but for the miracle of Dunkirk.

The German advance continued at lightning speed across France and Anglo-French relations deteriorated. Churchill flew to France on three separate occasions to encourage the French leaders to keep fighting. He also sent another expeditionary force over to France under the command of General Brooke. When there was a plan for the latter to return, Churchill telephoned him to say he must stay to support the French Army. Brooke replied that it was impossible to support a corpse. He thought it wrong to waste his soldiers' lives to no avail when they were so badly needed to defend England. After a fierce and prolonged argument, the first of many in the years ahead, Churchill accepted Brooke's advice. Around 191,000 troops returned to Britain.

A young and valiant French general named De Gaulle, who had been made a junior war minister, also escaped to England. He became the self-appointed Head of the Free French, entrusting himself with safeguarding the honour of France. Although a proud and prickly person who always had difficult relations with American President Franklin D. Roosevelt and Winston Churchill, he was a great leader.

The battle in France was now coming to an end. French armies were surrounded and they surrendered en masse. France's final surrender came on 18 June 1940. The victory in a mere six weeks was the greatest in Germany's history. Hitler thought of it in racial terms as a Mediterranean and Latin race succumbing to the superior dynamic master race. He saw France as a subordinate province of a thousand-year Reich, and a rich source of foodstuffs and slave labour. For a start, 1.5 million French prisoners of war were sent immediately to work in German factories.

The country was partitioned with the southern third left unoccupied but under a government at Vichy led by Marshal Pétain. Vichy France was under German domination and operated as an ally of that country and effectively an enemy of Britain. It blamed Britain for pushing them into the war and then abandoning them at Dunkirk. Neither of these seems a fair charge against their old ally. The French also resented the withdrawal of British fighter aircraft as airfields were being overrun and fighters were needed for home defence. The RAF losses of 930 aircraft helping to defend their country seem to have been overlooked.

Churchill acknowledged that despite the wonderful delivery at Dunkirk, we had suffered a colossal military disaster. When he took office he had said he had nothing to offer but 'blood, toil, tears and sweat'. Now, in another wonderful speech, he proclaimed in that famous growling voice:

> *We shall not flag or fail. We shall go on to the end. We shall fight in France, we shall fight on the seas and oceans, we shall fight with growing confidence and growing strength in the air, we shall defend our island, whatever the cost may be. We shall fight on the beaches, we shall fight on the landing grounds, we shall fight in the fields and on the streets, we shall fight in the hills: we shall never surrender.*

It is often said that Britain fought on alone. But this fails to recognise the enormous contribution of the countries of the British Empire. They were not compelled to join in and it was entirely their own decision to come to the mother country's aid. Their exploits were many and often magnificent. One should mention the Australian Army fighting so resolutely in many battles, and their particular heroism on the Kokoda Trail defending Port Moresby in New Guinea. The Eighth Army in North Africa and Italy included divisions from Canada, India, South Africa, New Zealand and Australia. New Zealand and Australian troops in particular played a major part in winning the Battle of Alamein. Men from all these nations fought in the Royal Air Force. The Royal Canadian Navy had a leading role in the Battle of the Atlantic; likewise, the Indian Army in Burma. The First Canadian Army together with the British Second Army formed the 21st Army Group in the invasion of France. There were also many volunteers from Norway, the Netherlands, Belgium and France who joined the fight. Polish airmen were particularly effective in the Battle of Britain.

Whilst we could not have done without these forces, from the outset Churchill believed that the key to eventual victory lay in persuading the United States to join the fray. Accordingly he kept bombarding President Roosevelt with messages seeking his involvement. The President, faced by the nation's strong isolationist convictions, had to tread very cautiously and was also doubtful about Britain's survival. Nevertheless, after Dunkirk he arranged the supply of large quantities of guns and ammunition to this country. This was the beginning of 'Lend-Lease', eventually approved by Congress, by which America provided equipment at a discounted cost on an interest-free loan. For the rest of the war we thus received many billions of dollars' worth of war supplies. But Lend-Lease was no charitable donation. Before agreeing to it, America insisted that we first exhaust all our foreign exchange and gold reserves, which were shipped over to the States. Our large companies in America were sold at knockdown prices. Great Britain became virtually bankrupt. It is also relevant that the 4.5 billion dollars that we paid in 1940 helped to rescue the United States from the Depression era and to prime its wartime boom economy.

Bankrupt or not, any doubts about Britain's determination were overcome by a tragic incident in July. It was feared with good reason that the French Navy might decide to join their new masters.

French capital ships in the Algerian port of Mers-El-Kébir were given an ultimatum. Either sail to America or Britain, or scuttle, otherwise face immediate destruction. Despite desperate pleading they refused, and British battleships reluctantly opened fire. The French ships were disabled and over 1,000 French sailors were killed. Not surprisingly, this hardened the enmity of the French Vichy government.

In July 1940, Churchill set up a large organisation to carry out sabotage and espionage in occupied Europe and to assist local resistance groups. It was called the Special Operations Executive (SOE). Many brave men and women acted as agents, and many gave their lives. One famous raid followed British concern that German scientists were experimenting with nuclear fission. Essential for their work was a supply of 'heavy water' produced at the Norsk Hydro plant in Norway. This was situated in a remote, heavily guarded and inaccessible position in the mountains. A brilliant operation by twelve courageous and determined men put it out of action and with it any Nazi hopes of producing a nuclear bomb. All twelve escaped. Their extraordinary achievement was made famous in the film *The Heroes of Telemark*.

Chapter 3

The Battle of Britain
Summer 1940

G ermany had for some time been planning a seaborne invasion of England. But without the necessary experience, equipment, or training in amphibious operations, and aware of Britain's great naval strength, they had serious doubts about its feasibility. The German general staff were reluctant. Hitler lacked his normal enthusiastic interest in the project. However, all were agreed that the first essential requirement was to defeat the RAF and achieve air superiority over the south of England and the Channel.

And so, on 8 August, the great Battle of Britain began. It was the first major battle between two air forces. Its outcome was critical for Britain. If this country lost there was at least the possibility of a seaborne invasion. If the RAF won, that threat was removed and the Germans would receive their first serious reverse.

Huge formations of German bombers protected by hundreds of fighters streamed across the Channel on a daily basis. Clear blue skies prevailed. The aim was to destroy the RAF and its airfields. Goering boasted, with some justification, that it would be over in a week. He controlled nearly 2,000 bombers and about 900 fighter aircraft (ME 109s). These were fine aircraft but with a short range. Once over the Channel they could fight for only about twenty minutes before returning. After suffering heavy losses in France, Britain had only about 600 or 700 Spitfires and Hurricanes. About a third of the RAF's pilots came from Poland, the Commonwealth and other countries. But many from this country were young and inexperienced 19 to 22-year-olds, rushed from flying school after only an inadequate twenty hours' flying training. Fighter Command was led by Air Chief Marshal Sir Hugh Dowding.

Day after day the battle raged. On one bad August day Britain lost forty aircraft and twenty-seven pilots were killed. But German losses were usually considerably greater. UK aircraft factories, driven hard by Lord Beaverbrook, the vigorous Minister for Aircraft Production, were building from 400 to 500 planes a month – many more than were lost.

The British invention of radar in the 1930s was of the highest importance. Radar stations along the south coast provided excellent air warning information about approaching enemy formations. This allowed the avoidance of wasteful air patrols over the Channel. It also enabled fighters to be accurately deployed and the pilots kept briefed as the situation changed. Just as radar was to be a major factor in the Battle of the Atlantic, so it was in the Battle of Britain.

At the end of August, as the enemy continued to pour bomber formations over the Channel, the German Navy was collecting hundreds of flat-bottomed boats and barges. They hoped to launch an invasion before autumn weather made the Channel effectively impassable. The tide of battle was turning against this country. More and more airfields and their facilities suffered major damage and became at least temporarily out of action. Pilots flying several sorties a day were becoming increasingly exhausted. They fought on with unsurpassed gallantry, but their great courage could not prevent heavy casualties. On 31 August, thirty-nine pilots were killed. Altogether in August, Britain lost 304 pilots and only 260 replacements completed their training.

Then, in early September, Hitler made another of his great strategic errors. Infuriated by British bomber attacks on Berlin, he ordered the Luftwaffe to switch its target to London. Massive raids brought devastation and huge fires to the capital. But before the attack returned to airfields, many facilities and aircraft could be repaired and runways returned to use. Above all, pilots could have a brief rest from constant fear and exhaustion.

Although the Germans returned to targeting airfields with raids of over a thousand bombers, it was a major turning point. The end was coming closer. On 15 September, twenty-three squadrons of Spitfires and Hurricanes were scrambled to meet another major assault. People all over Kent watched the dogfight vapour trails swirling above them and cheered whenever a bomber came crashing down. By the end of the day, Britain had lost twenty-seven aircraft with twelve pilots killed. But fifty-six German aircraft and many pilots failed to return.

The battle was now virtually over. Although the RAF had lost 723 aircraft, the Luftwaffe had lost over 2,000. Hitler cancelled plans for Operation Sea Lion, the invasion of England, and they were never revived. The United Kingdom had won one of the most important battles in its history. Churchill famously summed it up: 'Never in the field of human conflict was so much owed by so many to so few.'

Chapter 4

The Blitz and Wartime Great Britain

From September 1940 to May 1941, Hitler carried out the systematic bombing of London and several major cities. This was known as the Blitz. Night after night, people slept in makeshift shelters or in cellars or underground stations. Anti-aircraft defences and night fighter aircraft could do little to stem the rain of bombs. Many were incendiaries causing huge fires. The red sky above the fire of London was visible from 30 miles away. Including lesser attacks later in the war, nearly 100,000 civilians in London and other cities were killed or injured. About 300,000 houses were destroyed or badly damaged. Many other major towns were badly hit, Coventry being one of the worst. But looking at the big picture, despite the many individual tragedies involved, the Blitz had little serious effect on Britain's ability to continue the war. Churchill contributed greatly to maintaining civilian morale and was widely admired. He was cheered when touring bomb sites or appearing in cinema news pictures.

Apart from the Blitz, life was fairly grim for everyone. Air raid wardens enforced a complete blackout. You were in trouble if they spotted a glow through the curtains or a chink of light between the blackout screens. Food rationing was severe. For instance, 2oz

(57gm) of butter per person a week did not go very far, especially as margarine in those days was an ill-tasting substitute also in short supply. One egg and one rasher of bacon a week was also the rule. It is hard to forget the taste of rhubarb jam. Many basic foods such as fruit and cereals were usually unobtainable. Much else was rationed, including petrol, clothes and many household items such as soap. Seven million acres of grassland were ploughed up to increase home food production and householders everywhere followed the call 'Dig For Victory'. There is a nice story about four patriotic children faced with only three buns. One of them chanted:

Long to reign over us
Three buns 'tween four of us
Thank the Lord there's no more of us
God Save the King

In those days, Great Britain was a surprisingly ill-educated nation. Ninety per cent of children left school at fourteen. The services had problems teaching recruits their basic military tasks. One million men were unemployed.

In 1940, emergency laws were passed giving the state dictatorial powers, which were forcefully used. Anyone spreading rumours or misinformation that could damage morale was liable to prosecution. Press freedom was severely limited. Suspected Nazi sympathisers could be arrested and detained without trial. Conscription was introduced early in the war. This included the enlistment of women.

Many joined the forces. Eventually, 7 million women became part of a major labour force in the factories, the nation's transport and civil defence, and in the Women's Land Army to keep our farms producing food. Conscription was eventually extended to men up to the age of sixty, but many in 'reserved' occupations such as railwaymen, farmers, merchant seamen, police, were not called up. Government regulations governed everyone's lives. The Minister of Labour, the redoubtable Ernest Bevin, had the authority to direct any person to any job. It had become a people's war with almost everybody from eighteen to seventy involved in one way or another.

Volunteers were called to enlist in the Home Guard and one and a half million men, elderly or in reserved occupations, answered the call. As parodied in the TV series *Dad's Army*, they were initially armed mainly with pitchforks and a few shotguns. But eventually they became a properly trained and armed last-ditch defence force serving their country well.

To escape the bombing, a million young children were evacuated to the countryside. There they lived with strangers. Many had happy experiences and were well looked after, but a substantial number deeply missed their parents and remained very unhappy.

Despite all this, civilian morale, though sometimes bent and battered, never collapsed. It was supported by effective government propaganda and partial control of news, together with Churchill's great speeches. Army victories were trumpeted and reverses kept metaphorically in small print. This was in some contrast to

Germany. There the Minister of Propaganda Joseph Goebbels led a large organisation completely controlling all public information. A constant stream of outright lies helped the Gestapo keep the German public onside. One of the broadcasters who delivered outrageous lies in English was William Joyce. He was born in America but subsequently lived in Ireland and England, and had a British passport. His broadcasts were widely derided in Great Britain, and he became a joke and was nicknamed 'Lord Haw Haw'. In 1946, he was arrested, found guilty of treason and executed.

It was enormously valuable that by 1941, Winston Churchill had established a close personal relationship with President Roosevelt. In January 1941, the President sent a handwritten message to Churchill in London. It was a verse from Longfellow:

Sail on O Ship of State
Sail on O Union, strong and great
Humanity with all its fears
With all the hopes of future years
Is hanging breathless on thy fate

He added a comment: 'It applies to your people as it does to us.'

The two men had very different characters. Franklin Roosevelt was a great man able to display a warm charm. But many thought him to be essentially clever, cold, calculating and manipulative. He was supported by General George C. Marshall, Chairman of the US Joint Chiefs of Staff, a brilliant organiser and a man of strong character and integrity. Winston Churchill, like all successful politicians, could also be calculating and manipulative but was driven by his passionate patriotism and expansive emotions. A considerable historian, he was devoted to the British Empire. Roosevelt, General Marshall, and most senior American officers, always suspicious of British colonial intentions, thought this was an outdated institution and completely wrong. This fundamental difference often made relations between the two countries difficult and was the background to many fierce debates.

The President, encouraged by Churchill, understood that the defeat of Adolph Hitler was an essential interest of the United States. General Marshall agreed. But Roosevelt was faced with the majority of his countrymen being strongly against becoming engaged once again in a European war. Churchill was soon to have by his side an equally important figure to Marshall. General Sir Alan Brooke became chairman of the UK Chiefs of Staff in December 1941. Perhaps the most valuable British general of the war, he was a strategist, clever and brave enough to force Churchill to give up some of his wilder ideas. In his turn, Winston Churchill was great enough not to sack him despite their frequent stormy disagreements. With the strategic views of the two countries often widely divergent, it is much to the credit of their political and military leaders that agreement was always reached in the end. Meanwhile, the President was slowly edging his country into the war.

In May 1941, there was a bizarre incident involving Deputy Führer Rudolf Hess, who had been close to Hitler in the 1930s but was now much less powerful. Although still a strongly committed Nazi, Hess felt that Germany and Britain were natural allies and should make peace. He had a somewhat ridiculous belief that this might be achieved by negotiations with a Scottish landowner, the Duke of Hamilton. Without telling anyone, he made a remarkable five-hour flight in a Messerschmitt with long-range tanks and parachuted into Scotland. He was immediately arrested and imprisoned. Hitler was appalled and consternation reigned in the Reich. Goebbels quickly spread the story that Hess was mentally ill, which was at least partly true. Stalin believed it was an attempt by Germany and Britain to form an anti-Bolshevik partnership against the Soviet Union. After the war, Hess was convicted of war crimes and sentenced to life imprisonment. Always erratic in his mental state, he died in prison at the age of ninety-three after several failed suicide attempts. A sad figure.

In August 1941, the Canadian island province of Newfoundland saw the first of many meetings between President Roosevelt, Winston Churchill, and their respective staffs. A good rapport and personal friendship between the two leaders and between some of their senior officers was quickly established. The meeting produced the 'Atlantic Charter', an idealistic statement of Allied war aims. The charter emphasised that the Allies intended no self-enrichment or territorial acquisitions. They would always aim to establish and support local democracy.

Chapter 5

The Mediterranean Theatre 1941 and 1942

In the summer of 1940, Benito Mussolini, the Italian Fascist dictator, decided to start war operations. First his aircraft bombed Malta, an important British air and naval base; with German aircraft later taking over, this was to continue for years. Then from his Libyan colony Mussolini attacked British forces that had advanced from Egypt. In October he invaded Greece. The Italian Army, though not lacking in courage, was ill-trained, ill-equipped, and not well led. Although Allied forces were heavily outnumbered, both assaults failed.

Britain's General Wavell counter-attacked. In two months his 7th Armoured Division, famously known as the Desert Rats, together with other forces, comprehensively destroyed an Italian army more than four times larger. They advanced 500 miles, occupied Cyrenaica, the eastern region of Libya, and took 130,000 prisoners.

At the same time, Wavell's forces from the Sudan and Kenya overwhelmed the Italian Empire's territories in East Africa.

The Royal Navy struck further blows. One might have expected the large Italian fleet based in the middle of the Mediterranean to have dominated their own sea. But crucially it lacked any aircraft carriers and in other respects was no match for the Royal Navy. In November 1940, the carrier HMS *Illustrious* launched Swordfish aircraft on a night raid against the Italian fleet in the port of Taranto, 170 miles away at the foot of Italy. The Swordfish were slow, obsolescent, open cockpit biplanes flown with great courage against powerful ship and shore AA defences. They put three battleships and a heavy cruiser out of action. Taranto marked the dethronement of the battleship as the arbiter of sea warfare and a new era of aircraft dominance. Then, in March 1941, the wounded Italian Navy attempted an offensive sweep in the Eastern Mediterranean. The British Fleet Commander, Admiral Cunningham, learnt of this plan through British decryption of Italian signal traffic. He led his fleet to intercept them. In a major battle off Cape Matapan, the Italians suffered a devastating defeat at the hands of three Royal Navy battleships. No British ship was damaged, but the Italian fleet lost three heavy cruisers, two destroyers, and 2,400 men. Their navy took no further effective part in the war.

But these happy successes on land and sea were not to continue. Hitler now felt he must support his ally. He despatched General Rommel to Tripoli with two Panzer divisions and other forces making up the 'Afrika Corps'. Erwin Rommel was a dynamic and personally brave commander who had made his name in the defeat of France. Then Hitler invaded Greece. Finally, in April 1941, to safeguard his southern flank, the Führer launched a savage invasion of Yugoslavia. The country was quickly subjugated and suffered

100,000 casualties. As many as 300,000 Yugoslavs were taken prisoner.

With a large German air force established on the airfields of Sicily and southern Italy, Germany enjoyed complete air superiority over the whole area. Merchant ships could no longer pass through the Mediterranean with any reasonable hope of survival. To supply the desert army from the UK, they had to undertake a voyage of something like 13,000 miles right round Africa, which might take two months. Obviously this was a colossal handicap.

The War Cabinet, in a serious strategic error, had earlier insisted on Wavell reinforcing Greece with half his forces, mostly Australians and New Zealanders. Completely outnumbered, they fought bravely but were soon overwhelmed by the German forces. After suffering heavy casualties, some 50,000 soldiers were evacuated by the Merchant Navy and Royal Navy, many being taken to Crete.

But this was not the end of disaster. A large German paratrooper army dropped on Crete. After fierce fighting and despite heavy German losses, poor command decisions led to our defeat. Once again, evacuation was needed. The navy had already suffered severe losses from German bombing. Army and air force leaders, fearful that the Mediterranean fleet might be destroyed, advocated surrender of our forces rather than attempted evacuation under constant air attack. But Admiral Cunningham (Commander-in-Chief Mediterranean) felt it was the navy's overpowering duty to support the army and refused to abandon them. He made a famous statement: 'General, you have said it will take three years to build a new fleet. I will tell you it would take 300 years to build a new tradition.' And so the remnants of our forces in Crete were brought back to Egypt. In the whole Greek and Crete campaign, the navy lost three cruisers, six destroyers and thousands of sailors; two battleships, an aircraft carrier, five cruisers, and seven destroyers were badly damaged. It was a heavy cost, but the navy had not let the army down.

In March 1941, General Rommel commenced his Libyan offensive against our Eighth Army. Whilst he was a clever and forceful commander, always wanting to go on the attack, he overreached himself on more than one occasion. In contrast with the British generals, he seemed to take little care of the lives of his soldiers. The German High Command, OKW (Oberkommando der Wehrmacht), often tried to restrain him but without success. He was one of Hitler's favourites.

General Wavell's forces were badly weakened by the reinforcement of Greece and by conducting important operations in Iraq, Syria and Iran to secure vital oil supplies. Rommel quickly won significant victories with his superior tanks and guns and advanced through Libya back to Egypt. General Wavell was a good general and a very fine man. But with insufficient forces he was quite unable to satisfy Churchill's incessant demands for offensive action. Churchill lost confidence and relieved him of his command in June 1941. The new C-in-C was General Auchinleck. Wavell became C-in-C of our forces in India.

However, not everything went Rommel's way. He launched a series of fierce assaults on the Libyan port of Tobruk, seen as a key to the Desert War. But tremendous defence by its mainly Australian garrison kept him at bay and a long siege started.

Our naval forces and submarines based on Malta sank many merchant ships crossing the Mediterranean to support the Afrika Corps. Rommel was constantly short of fuel and other crucial supplies needed to replace losses. The Eighth Army also had great supply and reinforcement problems. Only one or two small convoys with desperately needed tanks survived the passage of the Mediterranean.

At the end of 1941, naval disasters came thick and fast. In the Mediterranean, U-boats sank the battleship *Barham* and the carrier *Ark Royal*, while very brave Italian divers riding modified torpedoes put the two battleships in Alexandria – *Queen Elizabeth* and *Valiant* – out of action. Admiral Cunningham was left with virtually no fleet. Altogether during 1941, we had lost one battleship sunk and four badly damaged, one carrier sunk and two damaged, seven cruisers sunk and ten damaged, sixteen destroyers sunk and twelve damaged, five submarines sunk and three damaged. The once great Mediterranean fleet was now reduced to three light cruisers and a few destroyers. Admiral Somerville's Force H based at Gibraltar had one old battleship (*Malaya*), a small obsolete carrier and one cruiser. Nor could either admiral hope for replacements or for early restoration of damaged ships. The latter were mostly condemned to many weeks of repair in dockyards sometimes as far afield as North

America. Luckily, perhaps, the Italian Navy was in no mood to take advantage of Britain's extreme naval weakness in the Mediterranean.

Not surprisingly, the House of Commons was getting restive at the continual bad news, which now included the loss of the battleship *Prince of Wales* and the battle cruiser *Repulse* in the Far East. Churchill feared for his position after defeats in Greece, Crete, Singapore and the desert, plus the loss of capital ships and serious setbacks in the Battle of the Atlantic. However, in early 1942, at least some things improved. The brilliant but impetuous Erwin Rommel had overreached himself and General Auchinleck drove the Afrika Corps out of Cyrenaica again. It was a considerable victory, but he had now lost 800 tanks and 300 aircraft.

One of the army's major problems in all the war campaigns was the failure to produce a really effective anti-tank gun. The Germans had the superb 88 mm, which over the years destroyed thousands of British, US and Russian tanks. It was also an effective anti-aircraft gun.

An important success in the Desert War was the newly founded Special Air Service (SAS), which made daring raids behind enemy lines. Disbanded after the war, it was re-formed in the 1950s and remains a famous and effective special force with its motto 'Who dares wins'.

The see-saw war erupted again in the summer of 1942. Another Rommel offensive drove our forces all the way back into Egypt. In June, Tobruk was taken in one of our greatest defeats. Churchill was in Washington at this time and was distraught at the news. President Roosevelt immediately and generously diverted the supply of hundreds of guns and new Sherman tanks destined for his forces to reinforce the Eighth Army instead. That exhausted army formed a final defensive line at El Alamein, a small railway station less than 100 miles from Cairo. Auchinleck was sacked in his turn and General Bernard Montgomery took over the army. He was a very able, methodical and determined man who had raised the standards of every unit he had commanded. Although vain and difficult to work with, his clever personal PR efforts helped him to develop excellent relations with his troops. They liked and admired the positive and optimistic 'Monty', who made it absolutely clear that there was no possibility of any further retreat.

Rommel's exhausted army was still plagued by the shortages and uncertainties of his long supply lines. He now concentrated on establishing a strong defensive position behind an extensive minefield.

The next chapter of the Desert War, starting with a major Allied victory, is covered later on in this narrative.

Chapter 6

Battle of the Atlantic 1941 and 1942

For most of these years our war in the Mediterranean was going badly. In the case of the North Atlantic the story was even worse. The year 1941 continued to see heavy losses of Allied merchant ships. U-boat numbers were increasing whilst naval escorts were still few in number and lacking radar.

It is sometimes not understood that the submarine in the Second World War was a submersible rather than a true submarine. It was a torpedo boat that operated on the surface but could submerge to avoid detection. Once submerged and propelled by battery power, except for short periods it was restricted to walking speed and was semi-blind. The telescope was of limited use in typical Atlantic weather. Aircraft, particularly if they had radar, were exceptionally valuable in anti-submarine operations because they could effectively immobilise the U-boat by denying it the surface. Unfortunately, Coastal Command lacked modern long-range aircraft. Although now operating from Iceland and Canada they could not reach a central area in the North Atlantic known as 'the air gap'. Here the U-boats could operate with comparative freedom on the surface.

The inside of a U-boat was a cramped, wet and smelly place of great discomfort. In heavy seas the boat would be tossed around, causing further discomfort and occasional injury. Crews suffered the prolonged terror and danger of hours of being depth-charged. (Depth charges were basically large barrels of high explosive, dropped overboard by small ships, and set to explode at a particular depth.) There was the imminent possibility of death by slow suffocation or being blown to pieces.

As the number of U-boats increased, their commander, Admiral Karl Dönitz, was perfecting his 'wolfpack' tactics. Once a convoy was detected, over perhaps twenty-four hours or longer, a group of U-boats operating on the surface would be assembled ahead. Eventually the pack would launch a night attack together. They could then submerge for short periods to escape detection. It was an effective and murderous business, often in terrible weather.

The merchant seamen faced life in a sitting target waiting to be blown up and then being drowned or condemned to a slow icy death in a life raft, or worse, being burnt to death in a sea of blazing oil. Sometimes escorts could rescue survivors, but often they had to leave them to their fate as they hurried back to protect the rest of the convoy left sailing on unguarded. Many years later, Vice Admiral Sir Peter Gretton, who had been a highly decorated and successful escort force commander, described one such moment as 'my most painful memory of the war'.

The crew of a corvette not only faced mortal dangers but prolonged wet everywhere. They also endured cold, awful food and increasing exhaustion as they were tossed around in the stormy Atlantic, day after day, night after night. Corvettes were slow and outpaced by a U-boat on the surface. Despite their gallant efforts, in the first half of 1941 merchant ship losses were running at fifty or sixty a month.

During the year, British and Canadian naval forces gradually improved in numbers, equipment and training. The clever cryptologists at Bletchley Park, with Alan Turing in the van, started to decipher German naval signal traffic encoded by their Enigma machines. This was of enormous value. Convoys could often be routed round identified U-boat patrol areas. The priceless intelligence was called 'Ultra' and was treated with an exceptionally high level of security.

There was one bright light in the gathering gloom. In May, when the great battleship *Bismarck*, the pride of the Kriegsmarine, sortied out to join the attack on Atlantic shipping, she was soon detected. A gunnery duel developed with HMS *Hood*, a battlecruiser (fast battleship) of fairly similar size and armament, and the pride of the Royal Navy. But *Hood* was elderly and lacking in protective armour. A plunging shell exploded one of her main magazines and she quickly sank. There were only three survivors. But now, in a large operation, *Bismarck* was also doomed. Eventually found again by Coastal Command, she was torpedoed and damaged in a gallant attack by carrier-borne Swordfish aircraft. Limping towards Brest and safety, *Bismarck* was caught and surrounded by heavy warships that pounded her to destruction.

In the summer the Germans were seen to be building reinforced concrete U-boat pens at Lorient on the west coast of France. For the rest of the war these would give submarines immunity from air attack, but while under construction were highly vulnerable. The Admiralty asked Bomber Command to make them a priority target. But Air Marshal Harris was adamant in his refusal to divert any aircraft from bombing Germany.

Air power over the ocean was one of the critical factors in deciding whether Britain would win or lose the Battle of the Atlantic and eventually indeed the whole war. Throughout 1942, the Admiralty tried everything to persuade Harris to allow a few of his many long-range bombers to be converted to meet this need. But it was without success. Although the Chiefs of Staff tended to support the naval case, they appear to have been unable or unwilling to force the issue. Harris, with his argument that this would be a defensive rather than an offensive use of his aircraft, also retained Churchill's support. The historian Correlli Barnett wrote:

> *At issue then in the 'Battle of the Air' had been nothing less than Britain's very survival. This renders it the most important single British strategic debate of the war. It is, moreover, the one case where Britain's survival was imperilled not so much by enemy action in itself as by blind folly within Britain's own leadership.*

Much later, the need was met by American long-range Liberator aircraft.

In 1942, with the *Bismarck* sunk, the Kriegsmarine still had one battleship, the mighty *Tirpitz*. Particularly if based on the west coast of France, she could be a major threat to Atlantic convoys. There was just one dry dock big enough to support her and this was at St Nazaire, 5 miles up the Loire estuary. It was heavily guarded by shore artillery and AA batteries, and seemed impregnable. A very daring night commando raid was planned in which an old destroyer packed with delayed action explosives would ram the dock gates. Soon after midnight on 28 March 1942, HMS *Campbeltown* started up the estuary pretending to be a German destroyer. She was flanked by sixteen small motor launches with some more commandos. They were the means for carrying the force safely back to England. The deception did not last long before the shore batteries rained down shells. *Campbeltown* was damaged and most of the motor launches destroyed. But the destroyer pressed on and charged into the gates at 20 knots. Commandos disembarked and fought German soldiers as they sought to place further demolition charges. Facing 5,000 troops they were soon almost all killed or captured. At midday the Germans were inspecting *Campbeltown* when the planned enormous explosion erupted; 260 German soldiers were killed and the dry dock was wrecked. It was not used again in the war. British losses were 170 killed and 212 captured. There were other commando raids, but this was one of the most heroic and most successful: five Victoria Crosses were awarded, two of them posthumously.

The *Tirpitz* remained a significant naval threat from her base in Norway, where, over the years, she was repeatedly attacked and damaged by submarines and aircraft. These attacks included a particularly heroic operation by six midget submarines, each with a two-man crew. Four of these craft were lost, but two succeeded in placing charges against the battleship's hull, causing serious damage. *Tirpitz* was eventually destroyed by the RAF in November 1944.

Back now to the convoy scene. Altogether in 1941, some 500 merchant ships bringing critical supplies were sunk. Imports and oil stocks were seriously reduced. Churchill said later that the U-boat threat was the only thing that ever really frightened him during the war. Towards the end of the year, sinkings were reduced by Hitler unwisely ordering U-boat diversions to other areas, by terrible storms and by improvements in convoy defence. There was also one interesting minor success. Germany's most effective U-boat ace, Otto Kretschmer, who had sunk forty-six merchant ships, was captured when his submarine was sunk. He swam to the nearest destroyer still wearing his oak-leaved cap. His captor was Captain Donald Macintyre, a famously successful convoy escort commander, who relieved him of his fine German binoculars and used them himself for the duration. After the war he returned them to Kretschmer, who became an admiral in the peacetime German Navy.

In November, the highly decorated Admiral Sir Max Horton took over as C-in-C to run the battle. Possessing great energy and determination, his forceful leadership would in due course be brilliantly effective. But at this stage of the campaign any optimism was short lived. At the beginning of 1942, with America now fully in the war, Admiral Karl Dönitz sent his submarines across the Atlantic to attack their coastal traffic. The United States had failed to institute a convoy system and ships, particularly oil tankers, sailed independently and unprotected, silhouetted against the brightly lit coast. They suffered very heavy losses.

Then, in February, the Germans modified their Enigma cipher machines, and for most of the rest of the year Bletchley Park was unable to decipher the U-boat signal traffic. To make matters worse, the Germans cracked the British naval cipher used to promulgate convoy details. Although the Admiralty suspected that this was being read, its use was continued for the rest of the year. This was a surprising and serious mistake. In 1942, over a thousand merchant ships supplying the United Kingdom across the Atlantic were sunk. This outstripped the rate that replacement ships could be built. The government estimated that if this continued through 1943, the UK would run out of the food, fuel and supplies needed to continue the war. Defeat would have to be accepted. Whitehall was enveloped in deep gloom.

But then came brighter news.

In October, in the Mediterranean, a U-boat was forced to surface and, in danger of sinking, its crew abandoned ship. Lieutenant Fasson, Able Seaman Grazier, and 16-year-old canteen assistant Tommy Brown swam over from the attacking destroyer and started collecting codebooks and documents. When the submarine did sink, Fasson and Grazier were trapped below. But their courage resulted in a great breakthrough. The documents enabled Bletchley once again to start deciphering U-boat signal traffic. They were both awarded a posthumous George Cross, the highest award for gallantry 'not in the face of the enemy'. Rather unkindly, Tommy Brown was discharged for lying about his age. He deserved better.

We will leave that situation for now and look at what had been happening in the rest of the world.

Chapter 7

Germany Invades the Soviet Union (Operation Barbarossa)

itler's grand strategic plan from the start of the war was to knock out France and the United Kingdom and then concentrate on his great objective – the conquest of the huge Soviet Union. This had a number of aims that had been central to his thinking ever since he wrote *Mein Kampf*. It would complete the domination of Europe, the destruction of both Bolshevism and Jewry, and provide Germany with Lebensraum (living room). Vast quantities of grain and oil fuel would support the Reich, which was also desperately short of labour. This could be provided by a complete race of slaves – the despised Slavs.

It can be argued that two campaigns decided in the end whether Germany would be defeated. One was the Battle of the Atlantic. The other was Hitler's great attempt to conquer the Soviet Union, a nation with 193 million people, much larger than the United States. Fortunately, as strategists have pointed out, Hitler's grand plan contained some serious errors. For instance:

1. By failing to knock out the UK first, Germany operated on too many fronts.

2. Hitler failed to enlist Japan's help in attacking Siberia to divert major Russian forces and seize some of her huge fuel deposits.

3. Germany underrated the Soviet Union's vast reservoir of men and women, which enabled the Russian Army to recover from huge personnel and material losses. They also underrated the courage and toughness of the Russian soldiers. Often poorly led and poorly equipped, they fought fanatically to defend the motherland.

4. And lastly, like Napoleon, he took too little account of Generals 'Janvier' and 'Fevrier'. Optimistically believing the campaign would be over in about four months, German troops were not clothed or equipped to cope with the Russian winter.

On 21 June 1941, the invasion launched a genocidal war aimed at conquering the Soviet Union and exterminating 30 million of its citizens. It was to become a colossal clash of arms much greater and more terrible than anything before in the history of the world.

The German forces, the Wehrmacht, numbered about 4 million men, including a million in foreign contingents. They had 3,000 tanks, 3,000 aircraft and 7,000 field guns, with 600,000 horses. The Soviet Union also had millions of soldiers but they were not so well equipped or trained, and the Officer Corps still suffered from Stalin's earlier purges. In 1937/38, around 43,000 officers had been killed or imprisoned. They included three out of the five Soviet marshals, thirteen of the fifteen army commanders, and 167 out of 280 corps and divisional commanders. Their thousands of tanks were generally inferior, spread over a vast area and often ill prepared for action.

European Russia was split in two by a 200 mile wide impassable bog area called the Pripet Marshes. Hitler's broad plan was to attack north of this with Army Group North and Army Group Centre, and south of the marshes with Army Group South.

Army Group North aimed at capturing Leningrad. Army Group Centre would take Minsk, Smolensk and then Moscow. Army Group South would capture Kiev and the agricultural Ukraine, and then the Caucasus oil fields.

But first the Russian forces had to be defeated. This was to be accomplished by the Panzer divisions driving forward on narrow fronts and encircling large areas containing Russian armies whose men could then be killed or captured by bombing and attacks from all sides.

Perhaps Stalin was still obsessed with belief in the Nazi/Soviet pact. But it is difficult to understand why, with amazing obstinacy, he refused to believe an invasion was imminent even though this was well known and reported to him by US and UK intelligence agencies as well as by his own. His forces were positioned too near the frontier, unready and in hopeless defensive shape. They were quickly overwhelmed or bypassed and the Panzers raced eastward. On the first day some 1,800 Russian aircraft were destroyed, mostly still on the ground. The German infantry followed up, some mobilised, but mostly on foot in forced marches. Horses pulled the guns and supplies of fuel and ammunition.

After one week, Army Group Centre had surrounded and mostly captured about 400,000 Russian soldiers in the Minsk area. In two and a half weeks they advanced 400 miles whilst the Soviets lost nearly 5,000 tanks, 10,000 guns and again thousands of aircraft. Huge numbers of Russian prisoners of war were herded into barbed wire enclosures with no cover and little food or water. By the end of the war, out of a total 5.6 million Russian POWs, 3.3 million had died in captivity.

At first, Stalin was paralysed by shock. He retired to his dacha fearing he would be arrested and deposed. But his colleagues had no such intention. A new Supreme Command, the Stavka, was set up to direct the war, superior to all other government or party organisations. Five million people were called up immediately. By December, nearly 200 new divisions, averaging 11,000 men each, were considered ready for battle, albeit still very poorly equipped.

Meanwhile, as the weeks passed, the Russians fought back with fierce determination and enormous courage. Their fighting spirit, wherever in doubt, was reinforced by the commissars and NKVD secret police (predecessors to the KGB), who executed on the spot any who showed weakness or tried to desert. Stalin's iron law was that any surrender or unordered retreat was punishable by death. Many generals who lost a battle were executed. It is estimated that in 1942 and 1943, 157,000 Red Army soldiers were shot by their own side for desertion or cowardice – enough men for about thirteen divisions.

Spy mania prevailed in the Soviet Union. The NKVD instituted purges of the civilian population; thousands were arrested and shot. Lest they be released by the advancing Germans, the NKVD killed an estimated 20,000 prisoners in 1941. In an orgy of sadistic violence, many were tortured to death. Civilian casualties from bombing were very large. The Red Army operated a scorched earth policy, destroying anything of value to the enemy as they retreated. This together with the German seizure of food stocks to feed their armies resulted in starvation for thousands of the civilians left behind.

Fierce battles and the relentless German advance continued through the summer. In the Smolensk area determined Soviet counter-attacks delayed the Wehrmacht but hundreds of thousands of Russian soldiers were again encircled. As in other pockets, not all the soldiers were captured. Some broke out. Some joined partisan groups based in the forests who harassed German supply lines, attacked trains and railways, and caused further delays and dislocation.

The German Army was followed by death squads called Einsatzgruppen, directed by Reinhard Heydrich under the overall command of Heinrich Himmler. They were formed before the war as a security police force chiefly responsible for removing 'undesirables' from Germany. This involved the systemic murder of the physically or mentally handicapped and others such as gypsies. In the subjugation of Poland, their targets were members of the Polish intelligentsia and Jews. In Russia the targets were Jews and Communist officials. Needless to say, they committed awful atrocities. At Babi Yar near Kiev, they killed over 4,000 Jews in two days. The Wehrmacht were ordered by Hitler to support them. Some army officers were horrified, but steeped in their tradition of discipline and 'orders are orders', they generally cooperated, many with enthusiasm. It was not only Jews and Communists who suffered; villages were sacked and burnt, their Slavic inhabitants often enslaved or shot as partisans. Total Einsatzgruppen killings in the Soviet Union are estimated to have numbered over 2 million, including about 1.3 million Jews. After the war some eighteen Einsatzgruppen leaders were executed for crimes against humanity.

At first, many Russian civilians who suffered under Stalin's appalling regime welcomed their German conquerors, particularly in the Ukraine. But German atrocities soon undermined their enthusiasm. The doctrine of Lebensraum required mass execution or enslavement of the Slavs despite any military advantage that might be gained by their liberation. Himmler said that the purpose of the Russian campaign was to reduce the Slavic population by 30 million. By the end of the war he had nearly reached this target, with the final Soviet losses estimated at 27 million.

After two months, in late August 1941, it seemed that the Soviet Union had been overwhelmingly defeated. Half of its European territory and nearly half its people and production facilities were now in German hands. One unconfirmed statistic says that out of every hundred Russian teenage soldiers who started the war, only three survived to the end. However, while Soviet losses ran into millions, they were quickly replaced from her vast population. German supply lines of communication were by now very long and often disrupted by partisan attacks. The Wehrmacht had also suffered serious losses but these could not be quickly replaced. Many German soldiers were demoralised by the sheer scale of Russia. They had marched many hundreds of miles, crossed vast rivers and the endless steppes, swept by blizzards alternating with blistering heat. But their excellent training and exceptional discipline kept the armies going.

Early in the invasion, Stalin started an enormous logistical operation to move production far to the east out of danger. In six months, 2,600 industrial units were moved in 1.5 million railway wagons and trucks. Millions of workers followed. This huge operation enabled the production of many thousands of guns and aircraft as well as new and very superior T34 tanks. It was achieved mostly by women, living in makeshift accommodation and required to work eighteen hours a day, seven days a week.

Although the Second World War was fought in defence of democracy and civilisation, it contained a real paradox. The biggest victor was a dictator possibly even more brutal and ruthless than Hitler himself. In 1942, Joseph Stalin kept 4 million prisoners on hard labour in the Gulag, that large area of prisons in the frozen wilderness of Siberia. But had his savage dictatorship permitted the slightest backsliding, rational human beings could never have been persuaded to endure the hell of what he called the Great Patriotic War.

In August 1941, Hitler made a momentous decision to change his basic plan. Against the advice of his generals, he ordered reinforcement of the drive to capture Leningrad in the north and Kiev in the south. Both were at the expense of Army Group Centre. This seriously delayed the advance on Moscow, which was so important as the political, economic and rail centre of the Soviet Union. Some strategists suggest this decision altered the whole course of the war.

In the drive south, the Panzers once again surrounded and trapped several Red armies of perhaps 700,000 men. It was the largest encirclement in military history. Kiev was taken and the Germans reached Crimea.

But Army Group North was less successful. In a series of battles both sides suffered heavy losses. Stalin sent his most brilliant and ruthless General Zhukov, to defend Leningrad, where the civilians built 100km of earthworks and anti-tank ditches in front of their city. The German Army was stopped at the gates. Leningrad was surrounded and the terrible three-year siege started. By the end, about a million inhabitants had died, mostly from starvation.

It was about this time that the Soviet Baltic Fleet set sail with a convoy from Tallinn, capital of Estonia, evacuating 23,000 souls from that city. Minefields and Luftwaffe attacks sank sixty-five of the 200 ships that set out. This was one of Russia's greatest naval disasters.

In September, after a pause, a reinforced Army Group Centre resumed its advance on Moscow with forty-four infantry divisions, eight motorised divisions and fourteen Panzer divisions. They fought a series of battles and achieved further great encirclements. Once again, Zhukov was sent for to save the day. In October, he was greatly assisted by heavy rain, which turned roads and battlefields into a sea of mud. Movement of vehicles and guns became almost impossible and the advance stalled. Adolf Hitler had planned that by now the Red Army would be destroyed and the great cities of Leningrad and Moscow taken. But with a seemingly inexhaustible supply of fresh troops, the Red Army appeared indestructible.

Hitler believed absolutely in his own military ability and decided to take over personal command of the German armies. Eastern operations were now to be directed by him through OKH, the army's High Command. Responsibility for all other theatres remained with OKW, the top planning authority for all the armed forces, equivalent to the UK Chiefs of Staff. This resulted in an inefficient and sometimes chaotic competition for resources. It added to the widespread disorganisation already caused by rivalries between the various top power structures of the Third Reich.

Eventually the rains stopped and conditions improved. The German advance resumed against strong Russian resistance. Then

'General Winter' stepped in with snow and ice. Temperatures dropped to -40°C. Tank engines, weapons, artillery and railway engines all froze, and so sadly did the horses and soldiers. Most of the latter had no winter clothing and frostbite casualties exceeded those wounded in battle. At the beginning of December, with Moscow in sight, the advance came to a final halt. Fresh Russian troops now came forward. They were equipped with clothing, weapons and tanks all designed to cope with the extreme cold. They drove the Germans back and Moscow was saved. Although the German 1942 summer offensive was still to come, this was one of the turning points of the campaign.

Chapter 8

Royal Navy Arctic Convoys 1941–45

When Germany invaded Russia it became clear to Churchill that the best hope of eventually winning the war lay in supporting the Soviet Union, previously an ally of Britain's enemy. This view was supported by America, who immediately offered to supply material reinforcements. Unfortunately, only a trickle could go via the poor rail and road links through Iran. The main flow had to go by sea through the Arctic, close to German air and naval bases and within the striking range of German battleships in North Norway. And so the Royal Navy, although already short of escorts for the Atlantic, took on the task of planning and escorting convoys on this most desolate and dangerous route.

Convoys would be beset by pack ice, fog, ferocious storms and freezing temperatures while under constant menace of attack. Ice all over ships' superstructures led to the danger of capsizing. Sailors sometimes had to spend all night chipping it off. But despite all the immense difficulties, from August 1941 to the end of the war, a total of forty convoys carried 4 million tons of supplies to Russia. They included 5,000 tanks, over 7,000 aircraft, and many thousands of trucks.

At first, losses were few, but particularly in 1942, every convoy became a major battleground against U-boats and enemy aircraft. The distant support of the Home Fleet generally kept large German units at bay. But convoy destroyer escorts also had, at times, often with great gallantry, to drive off superior naval forces. However, merchant ship losses were heavy. In one April convoy, only seven ships out of twenty-four reached Russia. In May, another convoy lost eight merchant ships from the incessant air and U-boat attacks.

Then, in June1942, convoy PQ17 set out with thirty-six ships. At this time the C-in-C Home Fleet was already suffering from the Admiralty's back-seat driving in the form of tactical instructions being sent to convoys from 2,000 miles away. It was thus that PQ17 became a disaster. The First Sea Lord Admiral Pound, against the advice of his staff, overestimated the immediate threat of the German battleship *Tirpitz* and other heavy forces. He ordered the convoy to scatter and the escorts to withdraw to the west. This was a quite unprecedented and drastic decision, and was a death sentence for many. Individual unescorted merchant ships became sitting targets for German aircraft and U-boats. The escorts felt deeply ashamed at leaving their charges but had to obey orders. Twenty-three merchant ships were lost with their cargoes of 210 aircraft, 430 tanks, 3,350 vehicles and 100,000 tons of stores. Many sailors drowned in the icy seas and the Merchant Navy bitterly resented the Royal Navy's desertion.

After further losses, in September, convoys were temporarily suspended – much to Stalin's fury as his army was being forced back by the Wehrmacht summer offensive. However, the worst of the Arctic convoy losses was now over. For the rest of the war Germany's other commitments reduced their forces in North Norway and we lost comparatively few ships. In the winter darkness, however, the convoys continued their horrible journeys. Conditions in the escorts continued to be dreadful, icy cold, wet, and constantly harassed by the northern storms. When the exhausted crews eventually made their landfall at Murmansk, there was no warm welcome, nor any comfort or good treatment for the wounded – just bleak and Spartan accommodation, poor food and the surly, ungrateful face of Soviet officialdom.

In December 1943, a notable victory was scored when the German battleship *Scharnhorst* joined the attack and was sunk by the Home Fleet.

It is difficult to do justice to the stoic courage of our Arctic sailors. They contributed significantly to the Red Army's successes, which in turn supported the subsequent invasion of Europe. At least their devotion to duty was eventually recognised. After a long campaign by survivors, in 2013 they were awarded a medal, the Arctic Star. It could not have been more deserved.

Chapter 9

Japan Enters the War
December 1941 to June 1944

J apan had been at war with China since 1937, and by now had established control of much of her eastern seaboard and many of her industrial cities. China's experience had been terrible. She suffered mass starvation and there were many atrocities on both sides, including the Japanese massacre of 200,000 civilians after taking Nanking. However, the Chinese leader General Chiang Kai-shek continued to fight on through the war. This became a great service to the West, tying down a million Japanese troops. He was, of course, also fighting the communist revolutionary leader Mao Zedong. That struggle went on until 1949, when Mao finally prevailed and modern China was born. Meanwhile, in the three-way conflict it is estimated that 15 to 20 million Chinese died.

Chiang was supported by the United States, which established air bases in China and sent supplies in via the Burma Road from that country. The American general 'Vinegar' Joe Stilwell was appointed Chiang Kai-shek's Chief of Staff and commanded a Chinese army in Burma. He quarrelled with his boss and later refused to cooperate with the British, which much reduced the effectiveness of both forces.

Japanese military leaders dominated Emperor Hirohito and the government. After Japan made a neutrality pact with the Soviet Union in April 1941, the United States became the chief supporter and supplier to Japan's Chinese enemies. Thus the US became Japan's enemy too. When America, alarmed at Japan's invasion of Indochina, imposed an oil embargo, it was the final straw. Japan had already decided to embark on a war to possess the food, fuel and mineral riches of South East Asia. Agreement was obtained from the Nazi foreign minister that once Japan was at war with America, Germany would declare war and support them. Japan's plan was to start by inflicting major damage on the American Pacific Fleet in a surprise attack. Meanwhile, US politicians and military leaders gravely underestimated Japanese capability. Warning signs of imminent attack were not acted on. Complacency reigned.

On 7 December 1941 came the violent awakening. Without any declaration of war, Japan launched a mass air attack on America's major base Pearl Harbour in Hawaii. It was a sleepy Sunday morning when 180 aircraft, launched from six Japanese aircraft carriers, made their attack. In two hours, the United States lost four battleships, with three others seriously damaged, and three cruisers. Hundreds of US aircraft parked together in the open were destroyed. A total of 2,403 Americans died and another thousand were wounded. A naval disaster indeed, but with one big saving grace: the US Navy's three aircraft carriers were hundreds of miles away and unharmed. They would subsequently prove to be much more important than the battleships. Although the attack brought

Japan short-term gains, by uniting Americans behind the war effort it caused her certain eventual defeat.

A whole nation awoke in fury and reacted fast. America's massive economy and all means of production were taken under state control. Conscription was introduced, taxation sharply raised, rationing imposed, and civilian car production completely halted in favour of military vehicles. The USN Admiral Nimitz became the excellent new C-in-C Pacific Fleet and Admiral Ernest King became the Chief of Naval Operations in Washington, in charge of the whole US Navy. A fiercely abrasive man, he disapproved of the UK/US agreement that the first priority of the Allies was the defeat of Germany, and he did not always follow it. Admiral King disliked the British, who complained of his prejudice. American senior officers replied that he was not prejudiced; he hated everybody.

Hitler wished to support his ally. Also, as a matter of pride, he wished to declare war on the United States before that country declared war on Germany. Without consulting his military leaders, on 11 December he personally declared Germany to be at war with America. They were appalled. Taking on another major opponent seemed a senseless strategic error, particularly when his armies were being forced back from Moscow. Now, at last, the United States was fully joined in the war. Churchill, who had worked so long and hard to achieve this, was overjoyed. With the Russians becoming ever stronger and the Americans sure eventually to defeat Japan, he was confident that, provided

Britain did not lose the Battle of the Atlantic, the Allies would now win the war.

Churchill went to Washington to meet the President again and with their staffs discuss the new war situation. Close collaboration was confirmed and, very importantly, it was agreed that until Hitler was defeated, the European war should have overriding priority.

As some eye-watering statistics demonstrate, UK confidence in the mighty economic power of the US was not misplaced. By the end of the war she had produced 296,000 aircraft, 350 million tons of bombs, 88,000 landing craft, 12 million rifles and 86,000 tanks. Her shipyards had launched 147 aircraft carriers, 950 other warships, and over 5,000 merchant ships. A significant proportion of this colossal production was provided to her British and Russian allies, including, for instance, 800,000 trucks.

But all that was in the future. Japan was still fighting China, but had long planned this new war. Her vast military machine now moved at lightning speed. Following Pearl Harbour, Japanese bombers and Zero fighters attacked the US air base Clark Field in the Philippines and destroyed half the US Far East Air Force in forty-five minutes. By the end of December she had taken the British colony of Hong Kong, a number of US island bases, part of the Dutch East Indies (now Indonesia), and landed forces in Malaya.

The British battleship HMS *Prince of Wales*, accompanied by battle cruiser HMS *Repulse*, had been sent to the Far East at Churchill's insistence. Their job was to deter Japan, support the main naval base at Singapore, and defend Malaya against invasion as well as defend Australia if need be. On 11 December, they were operating off the east coast of Malaya unsupported by shore based fighters when a swarm of Japanese aircraft attacked. Both ships were quickly overwhelmed and sunk. It was one of the Royal Navy's greatest disasters.

London and Washington were stunned by the speed and ferocity of the Japanese forces as they smashed their way through South East Asia in one astounding victory after another. Now the main target of Japan's main army was the great Singapore fortress, defended by mainly British and Australian forces and believed to be impregnable. However, their commanders had greatly underestimated the Japanese ability to force their way down through the Malayan jungles and attack from the ill-defended north. Allied forces were poorly trained, poorly equipped, and poorly led. Morale was low. On 15 February 1942, more than 100,000 Allied troops surrendered to a force of about one fifth of that size and were marched into captivity. It was a humiliating disaster and a huge blow to the prestige of Britain and her army. The Japanese treated their British, Australian and Dutch prisoners with contemptuous barbarity. Many were forced to work in the jungle on building the infamous Burma Railway. This was started in 1942 and finished a year later, from Bangkok in Thailand to Burma, to support and supply Japanese forces invading Burma. Conditions were terrible. The half-starved prisoners, beset with dysentery and tropical diseases and with little or no medical aid, suffered very badly. However sick or exhausted they were in the fierce heat, the Japanese guards used torture and savage beatings to make them work harder. It is estimated that about 61,000 prisoners of war worked on the railway and about 16,000 died. The civilian labour force of perhaps 150,000 men suffered some 80,000 deaths.

US General MacArthur's defence of the Philippines provided a contrast to Singapore. His troops, the majority of whom were Filipino soldiers, were outnumbered four to one by the 200,000 Japanese invaders. Blockaded in the Bataan Peninsula and Corregidor Island, they fought with great bravery for four months until the starving remnants were forced to surrender. In Bataan, 70,000 already exhausted prisoners, ravaged by malaria, dysentery and dengue fever, were forced at bayonet point to march 60 miles to their prison camp. Denied food and tortured by thirst, they were treated with deliberate cruelty on what became known as 'The Bataan Death March', and 7,000 soldiers died before reaching camp. Thereafter hundreds died every day. It was one of many horrific examples of Japanese savagery.

MacArthur, personally ordered by the President to leave, made the simple but famous statement: 'I shall return.'

The Japanese continued their operations to capture most of the territories in the 4,000 mile wide area north of Australia, from the Solomon Islands to Sumatra. The Dutch East Indies (now Indonesia) suffered badly. When the capital Batavia was captured, 100,000 Dutch were marched off into vicious captivity. In Borneo and Java, almost all the white males were shot or decapitated. Many of their wives and daughters were gang raped and forced into prostitution in 'comfort houses'. During the war it is estimated that the Japanese Army press-ganged about 100,000 girls and young women into sexual slavery as prostitutes.

In February 1942, aircraft from the four Japanese carriers that attacked Pearl Harbour carried out the first of many bombing raids on Darwin, in Australia's Northern Territory. Much damage was done and eventually the naval base was put out of effective action. The raids reinforced the Australian government's serious disagreement with Allied strategy. They argued, without success, that it gave priority only to UK and US interests.

In less than three months, Japan had conquered most of South East Asia, a vast area rich in oil, minerals, rubber and food. With access across Thailand agreed with the Thai government, they now had their eyes on Burma, the gateway to India. Burma had useful natural resources of food, oil and valuable minerals, but possibly the biggest prize for Japan was the closing of the fabled 700 mile Burma Road. This led from halfway up Burma across the mountains to China, and was the only land access the West had to supply General Chiang Kai-shek's Nationalist China Army.

For years, Burma had been regarded as a remote and unimportant outpost of the British Empire. A country bigger than France and the Low Countries combined, its terrain and climate were regarded as its best defences. Vast tracts of dense, apparently impenetrable jungle covered steep mountain ridges, and great rivers straddled the country. There were few roads, monsoon rainfall reached 200 inches a year, and summer temperatures climbed to 46°C. The world's worst endemic tropical diseases were widely prevalent. Its military protection was provided by a mixture of poorly trained and ill-equipped British, Indian and Burmese troops, and to some extent by General Stilwell's Chinese army of 50,000 men. The British were brave but often homesick conscripts, while some of the Indians and Burmese had little wish to risk their lives to perpetuate the British Raj.

They were faced with a war machine of terrifying efficiency. On 22 January, Japan launched a full invasion with 35,000 men supported by tanks, artillery and aircraft. The Japanese troops were highly motivated, resilient, ruthless and fearless. They believed that there was no greater glory than to die honourably in the service of their semi-divine emperor. To be taken prisoner was a disgrace. The Allied troops, encumbered by heavy equipment, boots and helmets, found the jungle impenetrable and dangerous. The lightly dressed Japanese infantrymen carried their own ammunition and four-day ration packs, used bicycles or animals for transport, and slipped through the jungle like wraiths, often to make surprise attacks from the rear.

Rangoon was captured in March 1942, which allowed Japan to supply and reinforce her army by sea, pending completion of the Burma Railway. Allied forces, outnumbered and outfought, tried to coordinate operations with Stilwell's Chinese army. However, Stilwell hated the British and refused to cooperate. He carried out his own independent operations, which were unsuccessful and unhelpful.

The Japanese Air Force drove the RAF from their airfields and commanded the skies. After a disastrous defeat at the Sittang River, with heavy casualties and loss of equipment, the Burma Army faced being completely wiped out or escaping back to India before the torrential monsoon rain would bring movement to a halt in May. Lieutenant General William Slim was appointed corps commander to manage one of the longest retreats ever carried out by a British army. It was made in terrible conditions by demoralised soldiers, ill trained and ill-equipped, and heavily outnumbered by their efficient and savage enemy. On some occasions, wounded soldiers captured by the Japanese were tied to trees and used for bayonet practice.

Slim was an inspirational leader who had a great gift for communicating with his soldiers with humour and honest common sense. He was ready to speak personally to all in English, Gurkhali, Urdu, or Pashto, be it the divisional commander, junior clerk or soldier. As a result, even in dreadful adversity, he became extremely popular as 'Uncle Bill'. He was also a brilliant tactician, calm, resolute and widely read, with original, carefully thought-out ideas. Never vain and never showing despondency even in defeat, he was equally popular with his officers.

The campaign was eventually ended on the borders of India by the May monsoon. It was an ignominious defeat, but that the withdrawal was accomplished at all was a miracle of outstanding management and leadership. After heavy battle and disease casualties, less than half the army was saved, albeit exhausted beyond comprehension, with little or no equipment, uniform in tatters and many in bare feet. There were numerous stories of great bravery and endurance.

One of the consequences of the defeat in Burma was that the supply of rice to India became sharply reduced. Prices rose and regions that had a surplus, hoping for even higher prices, refused to sell to those such as Bengal with shortages. The cost became beyond the reach of the poor and the resulting huge famine lasted through 1942 and 1943. At least 1.5 million died. Lack of resistance to illness through malnourishment led to another 1.5 million dying from various diseases. Churchill, already angry with the Indian leaders who were demanding independence, refused to divert military effort to help the starving. This seemed a shameful blot on British rule. However, there was some recovery when Field Marshal Wavell became Viceroy in September 1943 and arranged a national plan to distribute food reserves.

The war in the Far East in 1942 and 1943 was much affected by personality clashes between American commanders. US Army Air Force General Chennault believed, and partly persuaded Washington, that his 14th Air Force could defeat Japan on its own. He quarrelled bitterly with General Stilwell. A similar impasse developed between the strategies advocated by General MacArthur and the naval C-in-C Admiral Nimitz. MacArthur was fixated on an army campaign to defeat the Japanese in New Guinea and the Philippines. Nimitz gave priority to advancing island group by island group towards Japan, and cutting off all supplies to far-flung garrisons. With MacArthur's grip on the press and public opinion, Washington could not resolve this difference and allowed a 'Twin Axis' policy to be followed. Only America's ability to produce enormous numbers of ships and aircraft made this possible. In both strategies it was the contest between Japanese and American aircraft carriers that would decide whether or not Japan could maintain her command over the vast areas of South East Asia. Both sides were short of these great ships whose aircraft ruled the skies. But America was building them much faster than Japan.

In May 1942, Japan assembled an invasion force to take New Guinea and Papua, which would then threaten an attack on Australia. Ahead of the invasion force an indecisive naval battle took place in the Coral Sea. The United States lost the carrier *Lexington* and had *Yorktown* damaged. One Japanese carrier was sunk and two damaged, and the invasion was called off.

Japanese Admiral Isoroku Yamamoto now turned his attention to the US air and naval base on the island of Midway, some 1,500 miles from Pearl Harbour. This could provide Japan with a base for attacking Pearl Harbour again, leaving the United States with no Pacific base outside Australia. Midway was thus of great strategic importance. Yamamoto secretly assembled an armada of 164 ships to launch the invasion. One section of this force, some distance away from the others, included his four operational carriers. He believed the Americans only had two carriers, neither within 1,000 miles of Midway. But he was wrong. American cryptographers had broken a Japanese naval cipher and learnt of their enemy's intentions. The aircraft carriers *Enterprise*, *Hornet* and the rapidly repaired *Yorktown* raced to protect the island base. On 4 June, Japanese carriers launched their first attack against the defences of Midway with some success. Midway-based aircraft then counter-attacked but achieved little and suffered heavy losses. The US carriers then launched their slow 'Devastator' torpedo bombers to attack the enemy carriers over 200 miles away. This attack was a complete and tragic failure, with almost all the planes shot down by Zero fighter aircraft. Many of the young American pilots were only just out of flying school but they fought with great courage. It was bad enough to be shot down over the sea, but to be picked up by a Japanese warship meant almost certain execution by beheading.

The crews of the Japanese carriers were jubilant, convinced victory was near as they prepared to make another attack. First they had to recover, rearm and refuel their returning bombers and Zero fighters, and then arm all their reserve aircraft. Decisions were made about which plane would carry bombs and which would be armed with torpedoes. Halfway through this process decisions were changed, causing further delays. Meanwhile, US carrier aircraft were on their way. Eventually all the available Japanese aircraft were ranged on deck, fully armed and fuelled, ready to go. There were also piles of bombs and torpedoes not yet stowed below. As the first planes started to take off, 'Dauntless' dive-bombers from the American carriers broke through the cloud overhead. They soon achieved direct hits on the crowded decks of three of the carriers, triggering further explosions. The result was carnage. Huge fires raged out of control, only to be extinguished as the ships slowly sank beneath the waves. The fourth aircraft carrier managed an attack that damaged *Yorktown* but was sunk the next day. The gallant *Yorktown*, once again on her way for repair, was later sunk by a Japanese submarine. Admiral Yamamoto called off the invasion. And so, with great skill and courage, aided as often in war by some luck, America had achieved a colossal victory. For the loss of one carrier and 130 aircraft, they had destroyed four carriers and could thenceforth dominate the Far East oceans. The Japanese also lost 3,500 men and 275 aircraft. Midway was one of the great battles of history, and the turning point of the war in the Far East.

There were many further sea and air battles on a smaller scale. One of the most famous was on Guadalcanal, an island with a strategically important airfield under construction in the Solomon Islands. In August 1942, 11,000 US Marines landed and drove the defenders into the jungle, and then set up a defensive perimeter round the airfield. Japanese reinforcements were landed and soon launched a series of violent counter-attacks. In one such attack a thousand men charged American positions and 800 were killed. That night, the Marines huddled in their foxholes and listened to the crunching as crocodiles feasted on the bodies.

As the attacks continued, the greatly outnumbered US Marines carried out a long and heroic defence. It rightly became renowned in US military history. US General Puller, with defiant self-confidence, told his men: 'All right, they're on our left, they're on our right, they're in front of us, they're behind us ... they can't get away this time.' Conditions were terrible as the rainy season downpours filled the weapon pits and men remained soaked to the skin for days on end. There were also many naval and air battles round the islands as both sides brought in reinforcements. Guadalcanal became a great trial of strength between America and Japan. Eventually, after four months, large numbers of new US forces were landed and the 1st US Marine Division was relieved. The brave Japanese troops, greatly weakened by starvation and heavy casualties, were overwhelmed. The American victory became famous.

Australian troops also fought heroically on the Kokoda Trail, which led to Port Moresby through the steamy rain-sodden jungles and mountains of Papua. They too were greatly outnumbered but they stemmed a major Japanese incursion aimed at taking the port, which would pose a threat to Australia. Both sides suffered horrible privations with no proper facilities for the sick or wounded. Eventually the Japanese supply system collapsed and some of their starving troops resorted to cannibalism as they retreated. By January 1943, with the aid of fresh US forces assembled by General

MacArthur, they were defeated and expelled. A British commander wrote that 'It was the Australians who first broke the invincibility of the Japanese Army.' This was deserved praise but might be contested by the US Marines.

MacArthur, considered by many to be a great general, was a forceful right-wing Republican who despised Roosevelt and ignored Democratic political authorities. Vain, and a master of PR, he was much admired by the American people and greatly disliked by the American admirals. During 1942 and 1943, he conducted many land operations in the areas around New Guinea and the Philippines. The US Navy provided support but concentrated on their campaign of island hopping across the Pacific with the US Marines. These amphibious operations led to many naval engagements in which both sides suffered big losses. The US forces developed a strategy of leapfrogging the more heavily defended islands, building airfields ahead, which enabled them to cut off supplies to the islands bypassed. The airfields, dynamited and bulldozed level by 'Seabee' construction battalions, could incredibly be made ready in ten days.

In March 1943, MacArthur's air force spotted a Japanese reinforcement convoy off New Guinea. There were eight troopships and eight destroyers. Medium bombers carried out a new technique of low-level skip bombing (further developed by the Dambusters in Europe). All the troopships and four of the destroyers were sunk. Actions such as these prevented supplies reaching many Japanese garrisons whose soldiers often starved.

There were minor engagements as well. One became famous. Torpedo boat PT-109, commanded by Lieutenant J.F. Kennedy, was rammed and sunk by the Japanese destroyer it was endeavouring to attack. Kennedy shepherded his surviving crew on a 3 mile swim to a neighbouring island, personally towing one of the wounded. They were subsequently rescued and Kennedy was decorated for his heroic leadership.

In April 1943, a radio message about a flight in the South West Pacific by Admiral Yamamoto was intercepted. The flight was ambushed. Eighteen Lightning aircraft fought off the Zeros escorting two bombers, one of which was carrying the Japanese Navy's C-in-C. Both were shot down. Yamamoto's charred body was found later by Japanese soldiers and given a state funeral in Tokyo.

In 1943, the balance of power in the Pacific gradually shifted in favour of the United States as the Japanese were pushed back. American advances were supported by a huge shipbuilding programme and the production of new aircraft such as the Lightning and the Corsair, which were superior to the previously dominant enemy Zeros. Throughout the Far East the Japanese always fought bravely. But their bestial cruelty to prisoners of war, to civilians, and to survivors at sea is still deeply shocking. It brought terrible torture and awful deaths to an estimated 5 million men, women and children. And it brought great shame on a supposedly civilised nation.

In Burma in 1942 and 1943, General Bill Slim was working up new divisions comprising many nationalities. He instituted a rigorous system of training in his own innovative techniques and tactics of jungle warfare, plus a relentless physical fitness regime for every man in his command. Humble, but always demanding high standards, his leadership continued to inspire all.

Attempts to drive the Japanese Army back achieved little in these years and the British resorted to a new form of warfare: long-range penetration jungle fighting behind enemy lines. Our forces, called Chindits, were commanded by a dynamic and amazingly unconventional leader, Brigadier Orde Wingate. He presented an unkempt, bearded figure, wearing his sola topi and sometimes walking around naked. He chewed raw onions, strained his tea through his socks, and at times hung an alarm clock on string round his neck. His troops were highly trained and subject to fierce discipline, which even included floggings and executions. They spent months of great hardship in the swamps and jungles controlled by the Japanese Army. Supplied by air drops, they harried and disrupted enemy operations, blew up bridges, and cut railway lines. Their casualties were many. Forced often to move fast to evade far superior forces, stragglers and wounded had to be left behind. Some agreed to be shot by their comrades to avoid capture and torture by the Japanese. Some were left with a weapon to end their lives themselves.

At the end of December 1943, the Burma Army commander, General Irwin, launched an attack into Arakan, the coastal strip. It became a costly failure. Slim's XV Corps was sent in very late in the day to try to save the situation but could only organise a withdrawal.

Irwin tried to blame Slim for the debacle but was himself sacked. Slim expected the same fate and remarked that they could now both go back to England and command platoons in the Home Guard. Instead the new Supreme Commander SE Asia, Admiral Mountbatten, appointed General Slim to form and command a huge new Fourteenth Army, eventually to number three-quarters of a million men from Britain, Africa, India, Nepal and Burma. He was charged, together with General Stilwell's Chinese army, to drive the Japanese out of Burma.

Above left and right: The Dunkirk Evacuation: in May 1940, 338,000 Allied soldiers, over one-third of them French, were brought back to Britain from France. They provided the basis of a new army and hope for the future.

Right: Adolf Hitler: the evil genius who started the most terrible of wars and whose arrogance and pride led to his defeat.

Above left: Winston Churchill: the difficult, emotional, impetuous, but truly great man who was able in the end to accept unwelcome advice, and whose inspirational leadership and drive led Great Britain to victory.

Above right: General Charles de Gaulle: the proud and prickly leader of the Free French after his country's defeat, often at odds with both Roosevelt and Churchill. Post-war, he became President of France.

Left: Air Chief Marshal Sir Hugh Dowding, Commander-in-Chief, Fighter Command. Known as 'Stuffy' Dowding, he was a calm, resolute, unemotional man whose leadership helped to win the Battle of Britain.

Reichsmarschall Hermann Goering: an ex- First World War fighter pilot, he became Hitler's deputy and head of the Luftwaffe. A vain, greedy, drug-taking, poor commander-in-chief.

The Observer Corp coupled with radar provided vital warning of air attacks and aircraft identification.

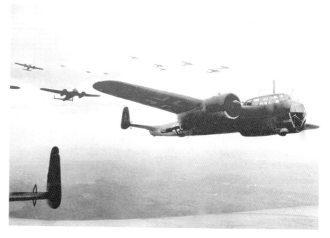

The Dornier DO17 twin-engine light bomber, with a maximum bomb load of 1,000 kilos, was the mainstay of Germany's air attacks on Britain in 1940 and 1941.

Nearly 3,000 Allied pilots fought in the Battle of Britain. Flying several sorties a day, their mental stress and physical exhaustion was always a worry. About 550 gave their lives.

The Spitfire – the 360mph fighter aircraft loved by pilots, which together with the Hurricane won the Battle of Britain. Over 20,000 were built.

The Messerschmitt Me 109, the backbone of the Luftwaffe's fighter force. Over 30,000 were built. Their speed slightly exceeded that of the Spitfire but the latter was more manoeuvrable.

Fire from incendiary bombs was a major threat during the deadly bombing raids on England in 1940 and 1941. Over 40,000 civilians were killed.

London was the main target during the Blitz, although many other cities suffered badly. Major parts of the capital were destroyed or seriously damaged.

An enormous magazine explosion marked the end of the battleship HMS *Barham* in the Mediterranean after being hit by one U-boat torpedo; 841 of her crew perished.

In many ways, Field Marshal Wavell, later Viceroy of India, was a great general in the Desert War. He also made mistakes, and could not get on with Churchill. He produced a wonderful poetry anthology, *Other Men's Flowers*, all of which he knew by heart.

Known from his initials as ABC, the highly decorated and fearsome Admiral of the Fleet Lord Cunningham proved a brilliant C-in-C Mediterranean and obtained major victories at Taranto and Mattapan. He was appointed First Sea Lord in 1943.

The Fairey Swordfish. Known as the 'stringbag', this mainstay of the Fleet Air Arm, though obsolescent in 1939, did great service including the attacks on the *Bismarck* and the sinking of Italian major warships at Taranto.

HMS *Ark Royal* – the best-known British aircraft carrier frequently claimed by Germany to be sunk. She was actually torpedoed and sunk by a U-boat in the Mediterranean in November 1941.

Known as Il Duce, Italian dictator Benito Mussolini entered the war on Germany's side in June 1940. He presided over many military disasters for his country and was eventually executed in April 1944 by communist partisans.

Admiral of the Fleet Sir Dudley Pound. He was First Sea Lord from July 1939 to September 1943, when he retired, and shortly after died. Respected for his hard work and good relations with Churchill, he will always be remembered for his disastrous decision on Convoy PQ17.

Above left: The depth charge was the principal but somewhat primitive anti-U-boat weapon for much of the war. Basically it consisted of a barrel of high explosive launched from the stern of a ship to explode at a set depth.

Above right: Grand Admiral Karl Donitz was the key German naval commander of the U-boat fleet who nearly won the Battle of the Atlantic (and hence the war). Eventually he commanded the whole Kriegsmarine and he led the German government after Hitler's death.

Below: The Royal Canadian Navy played a major part in the Battle of the Atlantic. Corvettes were small, slow, anti-submarine convoy escorts.

Above left: Alan Turing, the brilliant mathematician who led the codebreaking team at Bletchley Park and developed the machine that could facilitate deciphering German radio traffic. He helped greatly to win the war. Prosecuted for homosexual acts, he tragically committed suicide in 1952.

Above right: US Admiral Ernest J. King, the acerbic Fleet Admiral who became Chief of Naval Operations soon after Pearl Harbour, reporting directly to the President. Never a friend of the British, his daughter described him as even tempered, 'always in a rage'.

Below: The *Bismarck*. The *Bismarck* and the *Tirpitz* were two of the largest battleships in Europe. They were commissioned early in the war. On *Bismarck's* first foray into the Atlantic in May 1941, she was detected and eventually sunk by British forces, with heavy loss of life.

The obsolescent destroyer HMS *Campbeltown*, packed with high explosive and jammed on top of the St Nazaire dry dock gates, about to explode – the centrepiece of a brave and brilliant operation.

Field Marshal Sir Alan Brooke (later Lord Alanbrooke) Chief of the Imperial General Staff and from 1943 onwards Chairman of the Chiefs of Staff. His stormy partnership with Churchill led Britain to victory. Highly intelligent, determined and demanding, he was the greatest Allied general of the war.

Air Chief Marshal Sir Arthur 'Bomber Harris' was C-in-C of Bomber Command from February 1942 to the end of the war. He wrongly believed that aerial bombing could win the war on its own and, supported by Churchill, never changed his controversial policy, which did not include supporting the navy.

The German Tiger tank – a very large, complicated and expensive tank, which with its heavy armour and 88mm gun was very effective. Total production was quite small at under 2,000 units.

A medium tank, the Russian T34 was frequently redesigned. With its fire power, mobility and armoured protection, it was the most effective tank of the war; 80,000 were produced, with 45,000 lost.

As head of the SS, Reichsführer Heinrich Himmler had ultimate responsibility for the ruthless policing of Nazi Germany and for the Holocaust, as well as command of his own army, the Waffen SS. The most terrible German after Hitler, he committed suicide when in British custody.

Above left: Field Marshal Erich von Manstein, Germany's outstanding general in the Second World War. He planned the invasion of France via the Ardennes, and captured Sebastopol and recaptured Kharkov before being dismissed by Hitler.

Above right: Admiral Isoroku Yamamoto commanded the Japanese Navy. An experienced aircraft carrier captain, he understood the effectiveness of carrier operations. However, he wrongly believed Pearl Harbour might persuade the US to retire into neutrality. He was shot down and killed in 1943.

Below: Stalin, Roosevelt and Churchill: the Big Three first met together in Tehran in November 1943, then again at Yalta in February 1944. At the third meeting after the Europe War was over in July 1945, Stalin met the new leaders, President Harry S. Truman and Prime Minister Clement Attlee.

At almost every crisis in the eastern war, Stalin sent for the great Field Marshal Zhukov to rescue the situation. He was a brilliant and ruthless general who unusually stood up to Stalin successfully. After Stalin's death he arrested the dreaded Lavrentiy Beria and had him executed.

Seventy-eight Arctic convoys ploughed through the terrible conditions to Archangel and Murmansk with over 4 million tons of supplies, which included 7,000 aircraft and 5,000 tanks. Eighty-five merchant ships and seventeen Royal Navy warships were lost, although they accounted for about thirty U-boats.

The Russian Army was accustomed and equipped to operate in very low temperatures and snow. Surprisingly, the Wehrmacht was not and German soldiers suffered badly.

Above left: General Douglas MacArthur – a brave man with great powers of leadership, after a brilliant career. He commanded US forces in the SW Pacific and became the most famous of US generals. He was also vain and single-minded, perhaps narrow-minded, and could not get on with politicians or the US Navy.

Above right: US General George C. Marshall was Chairman of the Joint Chiefs and played a major part as Roosevelt's right-hand man. Although often opposed to British strategic proposals, he was a man of high integrity and a brilliant organiser. After the war, as Secretary of State, he developed the Marshall Plan to revive Western Europe.

Below: Japanese Mitsubishi Zero fighter aircraft. Introduced in 1940, the Zero was then the best aircraft carrier fighter in the world – highly manoeuvrable with a very long range. However, later in the war, US planes became more than a match. Ten thousand were built.

The US P38 Lightning aircraft – a twin-engine, high-speed fighter and fighter bomber with a long range. It proved very successful in the Pacific, downing over 1,800 Japanese aircraft.

With its crew of seven, from 1942 until the end of the war, the famous four-engine Avro Lancaster was the rugged and reliable mainstay of Bomber Command. Over 7,000 were built, and 156,000 sorties conducted, in which 3,249 of these aircraft were lost. Ten Victoria Crosses were awarded to crew members.

Major General Orde Wingate DSO and two bars – a brave, opinionated and highly eccentric leader known for his 'chindit' deep penetration operations into Japanese-held Burma. He was much admired by Churchill. In 1944 he was killed in an air crash.

Above left: A heavily decorated RFC pilot in the First World War, Charles Portal became Chief of the Air Staff early in the Second. He supported the strategic bombing campaign but had difficulty controlling Air Marshal Harris.

Above right: After notably brave service in the First World War, Field Marshal Sir Harold Alexander (later Earl Alexander) achieved a number of very senior appointments in the Second, culminating in Supreme Commander Mediterranean. Post-war he became Governor General of Canada, and finally UK Minister of Defence.

Below: Field Marshal Sir Bernard Montgomery (later Lord Montgomery) became famous as the Eighth Army Commander and victor of Alamein. Although vain, he had great powers of leadership, and was very successful in the Normandy landings and build-up he had helped to plan. Later he made some serious mistakes and was greatly disliked by his American allies.

General Montgomery led the Eighth Army in the Battle of El Alamein in October 1942, which saved Egypt and the Middle East and marked the beginning of the end for the Axis in North Africa. It was a long slog of twelve days, with the Allies losing over 1,000 tanks before they broke through, with Australian and New Zealand divisions in the lead.

The Consolidated B24 Liberator – the American heavy bomber and maritime patrol aircraft used increasingly in 1942 and 1943 by Coastal Command. Its long range enabled it to close the Mid Atlantic 'Gap' and make a major contribution to victory in the Battle of the Atlantic.

Captain F.J. 'Johnny' Walker CB DSO and three bars – an outstanding and much loved leader who commanded escorts and then a support group in the Battle of the Atlantic. Devising new tactics and sinking many submarines, he did more to defeat the U-boat menace than any other single officer. He died in 1944 of overwork and overstrain when about to be knighted.

Above left: General Dwight D. Eisenhower, the US Five Star General who commanded the forces for the invasion of North Africa and Sicily, and finally, France. Immensely capable, he showed great skill and patience in handling the challenging personalities of his commanders. Post-war he became the moderate conservative 34th President of the US.

Above right: Monte Cassino – a rocky hill in Italy topped by the great monastery founded by St Benedict, it dominated the Gustav Line held by the Germans. After several expensive and unsuccessful assaults it was bombed to destruction and eventually taken in May 1944 as the Line was broken, at a cost to the Allies of 55,000 casualties.

US General George S. Patton – a highly successful general in North Africa, Sicily and France. Famous for his hard-driving leadership and belief in rapid and aggressive offensive action, he was much respected by his German enemies.

Soldiers landing on D-Day. The US First Army landed on Omaha and Utah beaches, the British Second Army on Gold, Juno and Sword.

Royal Marine Commandos landing on Sword Beach. Together with other commandos, their mission was to reinforce the airborne troops holding bridges over the River Orne and the Caen Canal.

Field Marshal Von Rundstedt – one of Hitler's greatest generals, who was frequently sacked and reinstated by the Führer. He commanded an army group in the Nazi invasions of Poland and France, and Army Group South in the invasion of Russia. His last post was C-in-C West, where he was handicapped by a complex command structure that included Rommel and Hitler himself.

A German V-1 guided missile being brought down. Known as 'doodlebugs', their reign of terror against London started in June 1944. They contained 1,824lbs of high explosive and were primed to cut off the engine and dive to ground at a set distance from their northern Europe launch pads. As many as 13,000 were launched, killing over 5,000 and injuring 18,000, before their sites were overrun by Allied forces.

A V-2 rocket captured – the first ever supersonic ballistic missile. From September 1944, 1,359 were launched against London, causing about 2,700 deaths and widespread damage. Constructed using slave labour, the huge and expensive rocket weighed 13 tons and reached heights of 50 miles before plunging earthwards.

A V-1 direct hit on the Guards' Chapel. This occurred during the Sunday morning service on 18 June 1944. There were many casualties.

The V-2's 1 ton high explosive warhead damaged or wrecked many thousands of houses.

Admiral Sir Louis Mountbatten (later Admiral of the Fleet Earl Mountbatten). Promoted by Churchill to be Head of Combined Operations when comparatively young, he went on to be Supreme Commander of British forces in SE Asia, the last Viceroy of India, First Sea Lord and Chief of the Defence Staff. He was murdered by the IRA in 1979.

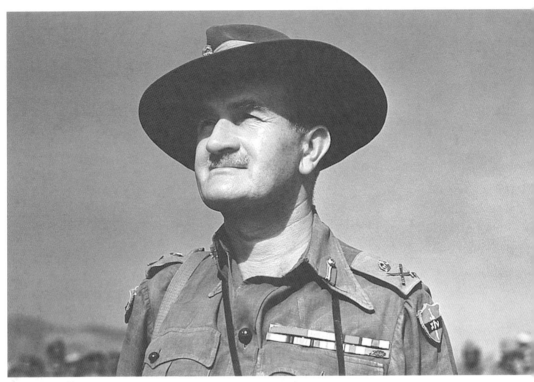

Above: Lieutenant General Sir William Slim (later Field Marshal Lord Slim) commanded the 14th Army – so-called 'Forgotten Army' – in Burma and in 1944 recaptured the country from a much larger Japanese army. Subsequently, he was Chief of the Imperial General Staff, and Governor General of Australia. Much liked and respected, he is widely thought to have been one of Britain's greatest generals.

Below: On 6 August 1945, a US bomber dropped an atom bomb on Hiroshima. Ninety per cent of the city was completely destroyed and 80,000 died, with a similar number dying later from injuries or radiation sickness. Japan surrendered on 15 August.

Chapter 10

The Holocaust

The Holocaust was the systematic attempt to exterminate the Jewish people in Europe. It was probably the greatest genocidal crime in history. This account will take refuge in being just a brief summary.

Hitler always intended to eliminate the Jews and talked about it often. At first he encouraged emigration and by 1939, about a quarter of a million Jews had left Germany to start a new life in countries all over the world.

They were the lucky ones. Once the war started, so did the killing. At first it was haphazard. Particularly in Poland, large numbers were murdered or confined to ghettos where they were later shot. In Russia, the Einsatzgruppen, together with the regular army, killed an estimated 1.3 million Jews.

Late in 1941, Hitler and Himmler decided that a proper plan was needed to organise the systematic elimination of European Jewry. Reichsführer Heinrich Himmler was in charge of the SS and all security organisations. His ruthlessly efficient deputy, Heydrich, was made responsible for implementing the policy. In January 1942, Heydrich chaired a famous meeting at Wannsee, near Berlin, where plans were thrashed out and extermination became official policy. The minutes did not use words like 'elimination' but used synonyms such as 'the final solution'.

Six extermination camps were set up with gas chambers. Train loads of Jews poured in. Some who were fit and able were kept for slave labour. A few were kept for terrible medical experiments by SS doctors. The rest were stripped and herded into the gas chambers, using whips, truncheons and savage dogs. After about twenty minutes, all were dead. Some Jews confined to various European ghettos were shot in situ. In April 1943, those in Warsaw commenced an armed uprising. They fought with suicidal bravery for nearly a month until finally overwhelmed; 56,000 were taken prisoner, 7,000 of these shot, and the rest sent to extermination camps or to slave labour, usually ending in death.

In the concentration camps German doctors carried out medical and surgical experiments on living inmates, often without anaesthesia. Diseases were injected, operations practised, and survivability examined in extremes of pressure and temperature. Over 12,000 died, often in great pain.

Heydrich was appointed as Reich Protector or dictator of the occupied Czech territories. Known as the 'Butcher of Prague', in May 1942 he was assassinated by Czech resistance fighters trained in Britain. The reprisals were terrible. In the village of Lidice the entire population was rounded up. The 173 men and teenage boys were shot, and the 198 women and children taken to extermination camps for execution. All buildings were burned to the ground and the village name removed from all records. Another fifty men, women and children from a nearby village were also killed.

In October 1943 and January 1944, Himmler addressed conferences of senior Nazi officials and officers to explain in plain words how the Jews, men, women and children, were being exterminated. None of these senior people could thereafter disclaim knowledge of the Holocaust. Overall it claimed about 6 million lives. It is a stark thought that this huge operation required the active cooperation of many thousands of German civilians. They included office administrators, railwaymen, police, camp guards, etc. Some may have had no choice, out of fear for the lives of themselves or their families. Some may have believed the propaganda that the Jews were just being resettled. A few helped to hide Jews at huge risk to themselves, but most seem to have been willing participants. One reserve police battalion, whose members represented a cross-section of German society, shot or deported to their deaths 83,000 Polish Jews. As far as is known, no one was coerced into their work or executed for refusing to kill mothers and children. Even when given a choice, very few declined. And so it must be said that whilst the Holocaust was mostly organised by the SS, responsibility for its implementation must also rest with a significant part of the German nation.

Chapter 11

UK Bomber Command

It may be that Churchill's pride in his warrior ancestry contributed to his strategies being generally based on a determination to take the offensive. However, these strategies were not always successful. As First Lord of the Admiralty he was the driving force behind Britain's defeat following the ineffective and expensive invasion of Norway. He also insisted initially on our anti-submarine destroyers energetically hunting U-boats in the wide ocean spaces, when they were only likely to be found near convoys. Against all senior military advice, he sought to add to the operations in Italy further invasions from the Eastern Mediterranean. These would have led to the invasion of France being cancelled or greatly delayed. Then, as already recounted, his desert generals found it difficult to cope with his repeated injunctions to attack before their forces were sufficiently equipped, trained and ready to do so. It is a mystery why such a brilliant man, an inspirational leader with great knowledge of war and long experience, appears not to have been a good strategist. Whether or not the operations of Bomber Command amounted to a poor strategy is still something that military historians debate. However, it can also be argued that Churchill's strong support for bomber operations arose from political rather than strategic considerations.

From the start, the German bombing of Warsaw, and Rotterdam, and later many British cities, was designed primarily to intimidate and kill civilians. The Allies followed suit. However, in the first year of war they were not well placed. Britain had only a small number of short-range bomber aircraft. Their bomb load was very limited, they had no bomb sight, and only very basic navigational aids. Not only were their daylight bombing raids ineffective, they also resulted in losses approaching 50 per cent of the aircraft involved. After the Battle of Britain the increasing numbers of twin-engine Wellington medium-range bombers improved things and a change was made to bombing by night. But the pilots were not well trained for this and their navigational aids were still primitive or non-existent. Photographic evidence showed that most bombs dropped at night in the first two and a half years of war missed their targets by several miles. But at least the raids showed that Britain was taking the fight to Germany. The inaccuracy was not public knowledge and national morale was boosted accordingly. But even in late 1944, if the skies were cloudy, 95 per cent of bombs fell more than a mile away from their target.

Daylight bombing eventually became the preserve of the US Army Air Force stationed in Britain. The famous large Flying Fortress bomber was the mainstay. It was complemented by the superb Mustang fighter, which with its Rolls-Royce engine, could also fly long distances providing protection. The Mustang was thus as important to the Americans as the Spitfire was to Britain. As many as 15,500 were built. This bombing was aimed at military targets such as oil installations and munitions factories, but if there was cloud the accuracy was little better than that of RAF Bomber Command.

By 1942, Britain had produced and developed a large new four-engine heavy bomber, the famous Lancaster. This became our primary bomber, and some 7,000 were built. Air Marshal Sir Arthur 'Bomber' Harris became the very forceful and single-minded leader of an increasingly powerful force. He had an unshakable belief that only Bomber Command could win the war and that everything else was secondary. The first 1,000 bomber raid took place in May 1942.

During that year it was clear that long-range aircraft were desperately needed to help stem our huge continuing losses in the Battle of the Atlantic. As recounted in an earlier chapter but also relevant here, all arguments and appeals to Bomber Command to transfer a few of their large force of long-range bombers to Coastal Command were absolutely refused. The Chiefs of Staff also believed that the production priority afforded bombers was excessive and was denuding the other services of much needed equipment. But they did not force the issue, probably because they knew that Churchill, who saw bombing as important in supporting Russia as well as the only way to attack Germany, would always support Harris.

One of the most famous exploits of Bomber Command was the 1943 audacious 'Dambusters' raid on three major dams in the Ruhr. It required very skilful flying. Nineteen Lancaster aircraft, each dropping their 'bouncing bomb' from a height of only 60 feet, achieved large breaches in two of the dams. The resultant flood damage to industrial production was significant but not major. Eight aircraft were lost, together with fifty-five out of 133 brave airmen. Their leader, Wing Commander Guy Gibson, was awarded the Victoria Cross for his own particular heroism.

As the war went on, our air raids became heavier and caused enormous destruction to German cities. Much has been written about two of them. In the summer of 1943, heavy raids on Hamburg caused a terrible firestorm, which reduced much of the city to ashes and killed about 40,000 people. It was said that the red glow in the sky could be seen 120 miles away. In February 1945, over a thousand bombers dropped nearly 3,000 tons of high explosive and incendiary bombs on the beautiful largely wooden city of Dresden, which housed many war industries. Another huge firestorm killed an estimated 30,000 inhabitants.

But the cost was high, with accidents making a big contribution. In 1941, for every bomber shot down, several were lost in accidents. The bomber crews were heroic. Night after night as they sat in their cold steel boxes, illuminated by searchlights and assailed by anti-aircraft batteries and night fighters, they faced the possibility, and eventually the likelihood, of violent death. They richly deserved the nineteen Victoria Crosses awarded. One in four aircrew came from overseas, and nearly 16,000 never went home. Altogether, 55,573 airmen died. This represented an appalling casualty rate of 44 per cent of all aircrew, the worst figures for any section of Allied forces.

Was it worth it? Arguments have raged over this. There is no doubt that the bombing considerably reduced the increase in German production that continued right until the end of the war. It never broke German civilian morale, but it did force Germany to spend a huge effort on anti-aircraft defences, including fighter aircraft greatly needed on the Russian front, and 50,000 anti-aircraft batteries.

Moral considerations in our bombing policy were given little if any weight. The prevailing axiom was that since Germany started it, they must reap the whirlwind. And indeed it was a whirlwind. Bombing led to the deaths of about 600,000 German, and 120,000 Italian and French civilians. Ever since the war, people have felt uneasy, if not sickened, by these numbers and the awful infernos that completely devastated cities. Others maintain that all war is terrible and that this aspect was indeed terrible but was justified.

Chapter 12

Soviet Union 1942 and Stalingrad

In January 1942, Stalin insisted on carrying out a widespread and ambitious offensive. It achieved some success in moving the front about 120 miles further west away from Moscow. However, in many of the battles the Germans suffered no serious defeat, although both sides had significant losses.

In the spring, the Wehrmacht was reinforced, re-equipped and revitalised. Hitler realised that Germany needed food and above all fuel to survive and fight the war. He now intended to consolidate his hold on Ukraine and seize the rich Caucasus oil fields east of the Black Sea. Accordingly, Army Group South was reinforced and a major offensive launched in May 1942. Much of the reinforcement involved Rumanian, Hungarian and Italian armies who eventually proved no match for the Russians.

Stalin, unaware of German intentions, simultaneously started a major new advance to retake the city of Kharkov. This was disastrous. Battered by the Luftwaffe, two Russian armies incurred heavy casualties and became surrounded; 240,000 men were taken prisoner and hundreds of tanks as well as 2,000 guns were lost. Stalin was enraged by this defeat and what he saw as a deliberate failure of support by America and Britain. Roosevelt unwisely encouraged

Stalin to expect an Allied invasion of France, 'the Second Front', in 1942. Although General Marshall pressed for this, it was ruled out by the British Chiefs of Staff, who knew it was completely impracticable. And then, as already recounted, the Arctic convoys were temporarily suspended.

In October, Churchill went to Moscow for a first meeting with Stalin, who was angry at the convoys' suspension and the postponement of a 'second front' in France. It was a stormy meeting. As a gesture, Churchill could only offer the bombing campaign and a major raid on the French port of Dieppe, which was about to take place. At times, Stalin became so bellicose and unpleasant that Churchill was only just dissuaded from walking out and leaving Moscow. Then Stalin changed course and invited his guest to a private supper. He became full of charm, understanding, and compliments. It seems that Churchill went home unwisely believing he had a new friend.

In the event, the Dieppe Raid was very badly planned and ended in catastrophe for the 50,000 Canadian and 1,000 British Commandos and American Rangers who took part. Within six hours of landing, three quarters of the force were killed, captured, or wounded and the remainder withdrew. Even if this landing had been successful, it was too small to achieve anything of consequence. But at least many lessons were learnt.

Meanwhile, the German offensive prospered despite Hitler's constant interference with military decisions. When faced with realistic situation reports it was recorded that 'he explodes in a fit of insane rage and hurls the gravest reproaches against his highly professional staff.' However, by the end of the summer, although weakened by the effort needed to take Sebastopol in Crimea, Hitler's army reached the Don and Volga rivers and the outskirts of Stalingrad. This was a large and strategically vital city, which stretched for 14 miles along the west bank of the Volga. This mighty river had an important north–south transport role. Not only was Stalingrad a gateway to the Soviet south, its name made it of high political importance to both sides. In August 1942, General Paulus, with his Sixth Army and the Fourth Panzer Army, was ordered to take the city. His force numbered about 280,000 men.

The Battle of Stalingrad started in September 1942 and went on for four months. It is considered to be one of the fiercest and most desperate battles in German history. Air and surface bombardment soon reduced much of the city to rubble. Tank operations were limited, and the battle was mostly fought at close quarters. Both sides showed enormous courage as they battled furiously street by street and house by house. Once again, Stalin sent Zhukov to take charge of the whole southern area. General Chuikov, the fearless leader in charge of the city, followed Stalin's July order summarised as 'Not One Step Back In Any Circumstances'. During the battle the NKVD division shot no less than 13,500 of their own soldiers who disobeyed.

After a month's fighting much of the city was taken, but heroic defence, particularly in the area dominated by three large reinforced concrete factories, kept Russian hopes alive. Every night, hundreds of wounded were evacuated and supplies ferried in across the Volga, nearly a mile wide, under constant bombardment. Soviet women soldiers and civilians fought as bravely as the men. In the whole of the Russian campaign (known as the 'Great Patriotic War') nearly half a million women fought in the front line.

As the battle raged, Zhukov had been assembling and training new tank armies in the east. In November, he masterminded a vast pincer movement north and south of Stalingrad using these armies. General Chuikov now retained only a small toehold on the west bank. However, Zhukov's new forces fought through the Romanian and Italian armies north-west and south-west of the city until, with great excitement, they joined. As the jaws closed, General Paulus and his men were trapped.

Hitler, who had now taken personal command of Army Group South, should have ordered Paulus to break out to the west through the thin arms of the pincer movement. But he was deceived by Goering's hopelessly over-optimistic assurance that his Luftwaffe could maintain supplies to the army by air, and by the prospect of relief by a new German army. He ordered General Paulus to stay put and continue the battle.

The new German army was mobilised but against tough Russian opposition failed to break through. During a terrible freezing December and January, the German armies inside Stalingrad gradually disintegrated in starvation, casualties, exhaustion and many suicides. At the end of January, against Hitler's repeated orders to fight to the death, they surrendered. Twenty-two generals and 91,000 soldiers shuffled off into Soviet captivity. They were all that was left of the 275,000 surrounded in November. After the war, only 9,000 returned to Germany.

In the Stalingrad campaign the Soviets lost 479,000 men killed or captured, and 651,000 sick or wounded. But they had scored a colossal victory. It signalled the beginning of the end of Hitler's attempt to conquer the Soviet Union.

Chapter 13

Malta, El Alamein and North Africa 1942–43

I n 1942, Malta was an important base for aircraft and for the submarines that continued to sink many of the ships supplying Rommel. Though eventually reinforced with some Spitfires, it was an easy target for the German bomber forces in Sicily and Southern Italy, and became the most heavily bombed place on earth. The Royal Navy suffered heavy casualties trying with scant success to force small supply convoys through. In March, one such convoy had all its seven ships sunk. The Governor, General Lord Gort, estimated that by the end of August, to avoid starvation, Malta would have to surrender. This would obviously have had very serious consequences for the Mediterranean war.

It was decided to try to fight a convoy through from Gibraltar with a large supporting force. It was called Operation Pedestal and became one of the most important convoy battles of the war. To protect fourteen merchant ships, the escort and support forces included four aircraft carriers, two battleships, seven cruisers, and thirty-three small ships. On 10 August, the convoy set out from Gibraltar. Soon the air onslaught began and went on day after day, with submarine attacks as well. In a long struggle, the navy lost one carrier with another damaged, two cruisers, and one destroyer with several more damaged. Nine merchant ships were sunk, but most importantly, five got through with 32,000 tons of vital supplies. They included the large tanker *Ohio*, heavily damaged but towed in by two destroyers with her cargo of 11,000 tons of fuel intact. She was greeted by thousands of people cheering from the ramparts and her captain was justly rewarded with the George Cross. Subsequently, the King also awarded the George Cross to Malta for the stalwart courage of its people.

Going back to the land war, in the late summer of 1942 General Montgomery faced Rommel's forces in the desert at El Alamein. He knew that, to save Egypt and the Middle East, he had to bring the Afrika Corps to a single great decisive battle and break its power for good. He obstinately refused Churchill's demands to attack until he was ready. Heavily reinforced with men, and with American tanks, he embarked on months of intensive training of his new mainly Commonwealth Eighth Army. It included divisions from Australia, New Zealand, South Africa and India. He personally devised and supervised this training.

Rommel, now a field marshal, had some 104,000 soldiers, half of them Italian, and 234 medium tanks. This compared with Montgomery's 195,000 troops and 910 tanks. It was generally agreed that an attacking force normally needed a three to one majority to achieve success. But other factors favoured Montgomery. The Desert Air Force, with many American aircraft, enjoyed air superiority. Montgomery also had the advantage of

Ultra. Most days he received intelligence based on the signals between Germany and Rommel deciphered by Bletchley Park. This gave him an exceptional understanding of Rommel's plans and intentions. Allied forces enjoyed this great advantage for the rest of the war in most land operations.

The Axis front line was defended by minefields over a mile in depth. Clearing a path through for the infantry would be a job for the Sappers (Royal Engineers) using primitive hand-held equipment, often under heavy fire. When the time came they worked at this task with immense bravery.

General Montgomery expected a long slogging match of ten days or more before the Afrika Corps would be finally defeated. On 23 October, he launched his assault, preceded by an enormous artillery bombardment. In the next six days, in many fierce engagements, Rommel held out so well that for a while it looked as if Montgomery might lose. But eventually the German line was broken and Eighth Army tanks poured through. They had heavy losses but so did Rommel's equally exhausted Panzer formations. Hitler sent a message ordering him to stand and if necessary die rather than retreat. After about eleven days, Rommel disregarded this, and to save the rest of his forces he ordered a general retreat. He had lost 20,000 killed or wounded, and around 1,000 guns and most of his tanks. A further 30,000 men and nine generals were captured. The Eighth Army suffered nearly 14,000 casualties, one fifth of them Australians. The 16,000 New Zealanders who fought so valiantly lost half their number, and 500 tanks had been put out of action. The Royal Artillery and the Desert Air Force played a major part in this victory.

Although it was on a small scale compared with the war in Russia, this was the Allies' first great land battle victory. After many defeats it saved the Middle East. No wonder Churchill ordered Britain's church bells to be rung in celebration. Monty was hailed with happy exaggeration to be our greatest field general since Wellington. Over the next six months, Rommel made several stands and counter-attacks but all to no avail. Montgomery pursued the Afrika Corps slowly but relentlessly all the way to Tunisia and their final surrender. He has since been much criticised for his caution and apparent lack of drive in this pursuit. It may be said in his defence that he cared for his soldiers and always tried to avoid unnecessary casualties. He was also very aware of the German habit of fierce and effective counter-attack. Finally he knew that the end result was inevitable unless he made some major mistake.

During 1942, there was serious strategic disagreement between America and Britain, which became evident at their leaders' meeting in Washington in June. General Marshall wanted to plan a 1943 invasion of France. General Brooke and Churchill thought this dangerously impractical, and likely to fail, particularly with the Battle of the Atlantic still in the balance. Instead, they argued for operations in the Mediterranean. There are many reasons for believing that the colossal Overlord operation of 1944 could not possibly have been mounted in 1943, and General Marshall's views seem surprisingly unrealistic. Eventually, Churchill persuaded

Roosevelt to agree with the UK. The President overruled Marshall and a very large Anglo/US invasion of western French North Africa was planned. This would open the Mediterranean and threaten Hitler's southern Europe while trying to allay Stalin's demands for a second front in France. It was called Operation Torch. It was to be commanded by the very inexperienced and recently promoted US General 'Ike' Eisenhower. A protégé of Marshall, he was a charismatic leader adept at maintaining relations between rival commanders such as the dynamic, vain, and intemperate General Patton and General Montgomery, who strongly disliked each other.

In November, the 33,000 US troops that landed on the Moroccan coast came directly from America. Some 80,000 men, about a third British and two-thirds American, had sailed 1,000 miles from Britain. They made landings on the French colonies of Morocco and Algeria, and were initially opposed by French troops loyal to the Vichy government. Not all the landings went well and the British casualties were heavy in their initial attempts to capture Algiers and Oran. Then, Marshal Pétain's Vichy government deputy in N. Africa, Admiral Darlan, signed an agreement ending French resistance. This enabled some support from Free French forces but it provoked the Germans into occupying the rest of France.

Operation Torch was at first a sorry story of inexperienced and ill-equipped troops, poor generalship, supply problems, and confusion between competing Free French and Vichy leaders, as well as between American and British army commanders. But after the initial failings and chaos at the landings, Allied forces gradually won the day. It is said, nevertheless, that if initially they had faced a German army rather than badly armed French troops, they would have been massacred. This was a sharp lesson for those who had been arguing for a 1943 cross-Channel invasion.

Hitler hoped to prevent the Allies establishing a strong base in Tunisia for future Mediterranean operations and sent in large numbers of reinforcements. The Axis advance along the Kasserine Pass in Tunisia was the first German encounter with the US Army in the war. The Americans suffered a major humiliating defeat by superior Panzer forces, but they eventually recovered and helped to prevent Rommel exploiting his initial success. Things further improved when General Patton was sent by Eisenhower to take over command. Britain's First Army also suffered serious reverses and heavy losses in the winter's drenching rain and mud.

In January 1943, another UK/US summit meeting was held, this time in Casablanca. Neither Eisenhower's report on the battles in Tunisia nor his plans for future operations went down well. He retreated from the meeting under much criticism, fearing he might be sacked. Many strategic arguments were repeated. General Brooke had been finding it exhaustingly difficult to restrain Churchill's strategic incontinence arising from his constant urge to be on the offensive. He was still talking about invading North Norway, the Balkans, and Sumatra in the Far East. These ambitions bore no relation to Britain's resources, particularly the limited shipping availability. Luckily the Americans refused to have anything to do with these ideas. They had other fish to fry. Admiral King argued as usual for greater priority in the war against Japan. General Marshall still surprisingly believed in a cross-Channel invasion of France (Operation Overlord) in 1943. General Brooke was determined that the next step should be to invade Sicily and seize its airfields. His views eventually prevailed and this was agreed. General Alexander was appointed to command all the ground forces, with Eisenhower the overall commander. In the hope of reassuring the suspicious Stalin, it was announced that the Allies intended to achieve nothing less than the unconditional surrender of both Germany and Japan.

As the months went by the situation improved. Aided by the Eighth Army's incursion into Tunisia from the east, and powerful operations by the Desert Air Force, Allied forces pushed the enemy back. Hitler, as at Stalingrad, refused Rommel's requests to evacuate Tunisia and save his forces. Eventually they were comprehensively defeated, and in May 1943 they surrendered; 230,000 prisoners were taken, half of them Italian, and over a thousand guns. It was another huge victory, which completed the campaign in North Africa and made it possible to invade Sicily and Italy.

In the summer of 1943, there were further summit meetings in Washington and Quebec. It was finally agreed that Overlord should take place in May 1944. The President obtained Churchill's agreement that an American should have overall command. As Churchill had previously promised this to General Brooke, the latter was deeply disappointed. In exchange Roosevelt agreed the setting up of South East Asia Command with the charming and glamorous Vice Admiral Lord Louis Mountbatten as Supreme

Commander, although Brooke had a low opinion of his ability. One of his deputies was to be US General Joe Stilwell, who hated the thought of serving under a British officer and loathed Mountbatten in particular. This would be more amusing were it not that men's lives depended on the leadership. The invasion of Italy was agreed and Churchill persuaded Roosevelt that the high secrets involved in the research and development of the atom bomb should be shared.

Chapter 14

The Battle of the Atlantic 1943
The Decisive Year

Up to now, Britain had just kept its head above water because of the huge United States production of standardised cargo 'Liberty' ships. The stage was now set, as 1943 opened, for the final, decisive struggle in the Atlantic. The result would decide whether the United Kingdom was realistically able to provide a base for an Allied invasion of Europe in 1944. It would also decide whether the country could feed its people, fuel its ships, aircraft, and industry, and continue the war at all.

It was a battle of technology, weapons, and intelligence. But ultimately the result depended on the willpower, decisions, courage and endurance of those who fought through the exhausting winter Atlantic storms. These continued at record levels into March.

At their Casablanca conference in January, Churchill and Roosevelt had ordered that 'the defeat of the U-boat must remain the first charge on the resources of the United Nations.' Unfortunately, some key Royal Air Force commanders took little notice of this policy. However, Coastal Command was now operating an increasing number of American long-range radar-fitted Liberator aircraft, a highly significant development.

In February and March, 128 merchant ships were lost in convoy battles. Very serious losses, but thirty-four U-boats were also destroyed – about half the total number operating in the Atlantic at any one time.

Churchill wrote: 'Never could we forget that everything happening elsewhere in the war depended on the outcome of this battle. We viewed its changing fortunes day by day with hope or apprehension.' In March 1943, as convoy followed convoy, most unharmed but some severely mauled, his apprehension must have been acute. It seemed that Great Britain was now in real danger of losing the war. However, the long-range Liberator aircraft were showing their effectiveness and some escort carriers (small aircraft carriers) could now be deployed in convoy support. More escorts were becoming available and levels of experience and efficiency were high. Some escorts could now be employed in support groups, available to go to the aid of a convoy whose escort needed strengthening.

One group of these was led by Captain 'Johnnie' Walker, who had commanded escorts right through the years. A fine leader, he devised some new and successful tactics, and sank many U-boats. The battle burned in him like a flame and he never left his exposed bridge for long. Eventually, exhausted by the strain of years of non-stop high intensity operations, he died. As well as the CBE (Commander of the Most Excellent Order of the British Empire), he had been awarded three DSOs (Distinguished Service Order) and three DSCs (Distinguished Service Cross). He was one of Britain's war heroes.

The turning point came at the beginning of May when a ferocious battle developed around the forty-two merchant ships of westward slow convoy ONS 5. It was faced with a concentration of about forty U-boats. In the end, twelve ships were sunk, but Admiral Dönitz lost seven of his precious submarines, with five more badly damaged. It was an unacceptable loss rate, which continued through the month. May's totals were thirty-four ships sunk, but no less than forty-one U-boats destroyed. Dönitz conceded that the battle was lost and he withdrew his submarines from the Atlantic.

And so, although convoy operations with some small losses were to continue to the end of the war, the Battle of the Atlantic was won. Altogether, Germany lost 783 submarines along with nearly 30,000 of their brave sailors. For every four going to sea in a U-boat, three died. Sadly, 35,000 Merchant Navy sailors also lost their lives.

It was probably Britain's greatest sea victory ever. It saved the UK from defeat, and it made possible the invasion of Europe. Allied forces on the Continent eventually amounted to over 5 million men and a million vehicles. All required extensive seagoing support. U-boats failed to have any significant effect on that landing or its subsequent supporting lifeline.

The cargo tonnage lost during the Battle of the Atlantic, as a percentage of the total import tonnage, was around 4 per cent in the early years, and peaked at 10 per cent in 1942 before reducing subsequently to 3 per cent or less. Some commentators suggest that these figures indicate that Britain's survival was never really in doubt. This view is reinforced by the fact that, overall, only 10 per cent of convoys were attacked, and their casualty rate was only about 10 per cent. However, it should be noted that despite strict rationing of food and fuel, the UK's imports were generally only just sufficient to feed the population and enable operations to continue. Should the awful figures for 1942 have continued or worsened in 1943, it seems the outcome would have become very seriously in doubt. Certainly that was the real fear of the government at the time.

Chapter 15

Sicily and Italy 1943–44

Britain's General Alexander had been appointed Supreme Commander in the Mediterranean theatre, and in July 1943 he directed the invasion of Sicily by Patton's US Fifth Army and Montgomery's Eighth Army. The battles here went on for over a month before victory was achieved. In Sicily and Italy the two nations' armies were always competitive rather than cooperative and General Alexander's most difficult task was to maintain some sort of reasonable relations between the two generals. In Sicily the Allies lost 17,000 men killed, captured or wounded. The Axis lost 164,000.

General Patton's brilliant career was seriously set back when he slapped and abused two shell-shocked GIs in hospital. He was removed from operational command and eventually overtaken by his friend and junior, Omar Bradley, who became his senior officer in the later landings on D-Day.

Churchill had been right to persuade Roosevelt to agree to Operation Torch and thus avoid the disaster of a calamitous cross-Channel invasion of France in 1943. But the central disagreement that had dogged UK/US relations since 1942 remained. Roosevelt and Marshall were determined that nothing should further delay that invasion (known as Overlord). Churchill and General Brooke gave priority to the Mediterranean and remained nervous about the possible failure of Overlord if the Germans were not further weakened. Churchill also became obsessed with the idea of retaking Rhodes and other islands in the Eastern Mediterranean. Brooke thought he had become completely unbalanced. Marshall suspected that Churchill secretly wished to develop plans for an invasion of the Balkans and refused to have anything to do with his wild ideas.

However, the conquest of Sicily opened up the Mediterranean as a valuable sea route, ending the necessity of taking supplies for Egypt all the way round Africa. This freed up about a million tons of shipping, always in seriously short supply and always a dominant factor in strategic decisions. It also led to the downfall of Mussolini and the surrender of the Italian armed forces. The Italian fleet successfully sailed to Britain's naval base in Malta. The opening of Sicilian air bases also greatly facilitated our bombing campaigns and provided useful air superiority over Italy.

Then, in September 1943, Allied forces invaded Italy. General Montgomery's Eighth Army landed on the foot and made good progress, capturing many airfields, which enabled Allied air superiority to be confirmed and a new bombing campaign against southern Germany initiated.

The American commander of the US Fifth Army was General Mark Clark, who outdid all the Allied generals in his personal vanity. He organised a PR staff of fifty people to ensure a constant flow of favourable publicity for his army and particularly for himself. His Fifth Army, which included a British corps, conducted a major landing in Salerno Bay, south of Naples. The German Army made violent counter-attacks and it was touch and go for a week whether the Allied forces would be thrown back into the sea. However, with massive naval gunfire support from the battleships *Valiant* and *Warspite*, plus air bombardment, they eventually won the day and broke out. The two armies joined forces, Naples was taken and a front established across the country with the Fifth Army on the left and the Eighth on the right or east. They now faced thirty-eight divisions of the Wehrmacht.

The German commander in Italy, Field Marshal Kesselring, reacted quickly to the Italian surrender. He seized control of Rome and other cities and sent over half a million Italian soldiers into Germany for forced labour.

Churchill misleadingly called the Balkans and Italy 'the soft underbelly of Europe'. In fact, Italy was a very hard nut to crack. With an Apennine backbone 4,000 feet high, 40 miles wide and 800 miles long, it was a country easily defended. In terrible weather that autumn and winter, the advance became a long, slow, exhausting slog. No sooner had one river or mountain been crossed than another barred the way. Air operations were severely limited.

South of Rome, the Germans built the 'Gustav Line' with deep concrete bunkers, anti-tank ditches, minefields, hidden artillery and 60,000 determined defenders. The line was dominated by the large ancient hilltop abbey of Monte Cassino (founded by St Benedict), which the Allies wrongly believed to be a fortress. Accordingly it was heavily bombed, almost to rubble. However, this simply gave the Germans the right to enter and turn it into a real fortress. The mountains on both sides of the peninsula overlooked coastal strips containing a number of large rivers, often in spate in the heavy rain, sweeping away pontoon bridges and assault boats. Over the winter the Gustav Line and Cassino became the scene of many fierce battles and many casualties for marginal gains. Both sides took few prisoners. An example is provided in two night attacks by the Royal Sussex Regiment in the unending rain and mud. Altogether, fifteen officers and 313 men took part, and twelve officers and 162 men were killed or wounded. A heavy price, but typical of hundreds of such attacks.

In the long and bloody stalemate, soldiers' health in both Allied armies deteriorated with pneumonia, fevers and dysentery. The debilitating infection called trench foot was rampant. There were thousands of casualties from sickness and disease, self-inflicted wounds and psychological collapse. Nearly 30,000 men deserted or went absent without leave from British and associated units. The Americans suffered similar problems. But the great majority of soldiers of the Fifth and Eighth armies fought on with stubborn courage in the cold and wet.

Montgomery's supply organisation was severely damaged in December when a German bombing raid sank seventeen ships in the port of Bari. They included one carrying 1,350 tons of mustard gas bombs, kept in case needed for retaliation. This ship and another close by carrying 5,000 tons of ammunition exploded and drenched the area in the terrible gas. Over a thousand soldiers and sailors died, as well as many Italians. Bari was out of action for two months.

In January 1944, a major landing was carried out at Anzio on the west coast, south of Rome. It was intended to outflank the Gustav Line and end the stalemate. It achieved surprise and within two days there were 50,000 troops ashore. However, the American general failed to break out and take advantage of the temporary German weakness. Kesselring quickly assembled thousands of reinforcements, and the Battle of Anzio itself became a stalemate and a very costly failure. In February 1944, Kesselring launched a new offensive with 125,000 men to drive General Clark's VI Corps back into the sea, but they held on, just. The Germans suffered heavy casualties from artillery and naval gunfire and called the operation off. Allied casualties were also heavy. In five days, a Sherwood Foresters battalion was reduced from 250 officers and men to only thirty. An Irish Guards battalion had taken 94 per cent casualties in the same period.

In May 1944, General Alexander launched a major offensive against the Gustav Line with nearly half a million men from ten different nations. The fierce German response was inevitable, but after a week of violent fighting the line was at last breached and they were in full retreat. Part of Alexander's plan was to use his forces at Anzio to cut off the German Army's retreat and capture many thousands. He ordered General Clark to break out east from Anzio and spring the trap. But Clark was obsessed with a great personal ambition to be the first to capture Rome and achieve fame thereby. Astonishingly, he disobeyed the order. He broke out, turned north, and on 5 June entered Rome, which by then had been evacuated by the Germans. The offensive to break the Gustav Line cost the Allies 44,000 casualties, a sacrifice that might have been justified if the German Tenth Army had been destroyed. But due to Clark's egomania it escaped and set up new fortified lines north of Rome, ready to cause the loss of thousands more Allied lives. It is surprising that General Clark was not relieved of his command, but at least his PR machinery could achieve no great success. Rome's capture was of little significance, particularly as it coincided with D-Day, the invasion of France.

As the fierce struggle up Italy continued, easily defended rivers and mountain passes were held with the Wehrmacht's usual ferocity and skill. General Alexander had seven of his divisions taken away to reinforce the troops in France. A long and bloody series of battles continued through another awful winter of rain, cold and mud. It was eleven months before the final German surrender, in the Po Valley on 2 May 1945. Altogether, the Italian campaign cost the Fifth Army 189,000 casualties, and the Eighth Army 123,000. German casualties were about 435,000.

Was it worth it? Could the Allied forces have been deployed more effectively elsewhere? Difficult questions to answer. But by occupying German armies that were much needed on the French and Russian fronts, these forces certainly made an important contribution to overall victory. At the same time perhaps they demonstrated yet again, as well as the huge human cost, the inescapable futility of war beside its tragic necessity.

Chapter 16

Soviet Union 1943 and 1944

Following victory at Stalingrad in January 1943, Stalin sent Zhukov, now promoted to Marshal, to coordinate the offensive to relieve the starving city of Leningrad. Using overwhelming numbers this was soon achieved.

Meanwhile, the Soviet armies of the South and Centre continued their advance and captured the strategically important city of Kharkov. But here they now faced possibly the most brilliant of German commanders, Field Marshal Erich von Manstein. Despite being greatly outnumbered, in a fierce counter-attack he retook the city and stabilised the front line. It was an impressive military achievement.

In April 1943, the Germans announced the discovery of mass graves in a forest called Katyn, near Smolensk. They contained the bodies of many thousands of Polish officers who had been executed by a shot in the head. The Russians claimed unconvincingly that it was a propaganda trick to conceal German guilt. Britain found it difficult to condemn this terrible massacre, not wishing to bedevil the already shaky relationship with Joseph Stalin. In all, 21,800 Polish officers were executed by the Russians at Katyn and elsewhere.

By mid 1943, the German Army in the Soviet Union had been severely weakened by its heavy casualties in all areas. This was compounded by the transfer of troops to Tunisia, where there were also big aircraft losses, also to France in case of an Allied invasion, and to Yugoslavia to reinforce the fight against Marshal Tito's partisans. Furthermore, the need to protect the Reich against Allied bombing led to the withdrawal of AA batteries and fighter squadrons from the Eastern Front, where Soviet Russia could now claim air superiority. At this time the German strength in the east stood at 2.7 million men against a Red Army of nearly 6 million, which also had four times as many tanks and guns.

That the Soviet Union could assemble and equip these enormous armies was helped by the Lend-Lease supplies brought in by the Arctic convoys. These included 1.5 million pairs of boots and huge quantities of food, arms and ammunition. But much larger amounts came from their own factories, with demanding targets ruthlessly imposed on every worker.

Despite his numerical inferiority, Hitler decided on a major offensive to retake a large western bulge in the Soviet front around Kursk, north of Kharkov. This bulge was nearly 100 miles deep and 150 miles wide. Ultra intelligence obtained from Bletchley Park soon made German intentions clear and the information was passed on to Moscow, as was the normal practice, without revealing the source. Once again, Zhukov was called for. He persuaded Stalin that the best way to defeat a new German offensive was to prepare well and fight a defensive battle. So both sides spent months preparing for the greatest tank battle in history.

The Red Army and 300,000 mobilised civilians constructed eight lines of defences with deep tank ditches, underground bunkers, minefields containing a million mines, and at least 3,000 miles of trenches. Individual Soviet soldiers were required to continue digging trenches every night. Altogether, 1.8 million Soviet troops faced about 850,000 Germans under the overall command of Manstein. He advised against the whole operation, but Hitler insisted that it should go ahead. The Germans assembled 3,000 tanks as the spearhead, led by the new huge Tigers. They faced an even greater number of Soviet T-34 tanks, supported by 20,000 field and anti-tank guns and the terrifying Katyusha mobile rocket launchers. The Soviets also assembled large numbers of ground-attack aircraft.

On 4 July 1943, the great German offensive was let loose. In ferocious exchanges day after day, their advance seemed remorseless. Red Army soldiers, warned of the German treatment of prisoners, were encouraged to fight to the death. After ten days, the climax came in a tank to tank fire fight between hundreds of tanks at close quarters. Here the Soviet Army came off best. Soon after, although the Germans had broken through much of the defences, their huge tank losses and the physical exhaustion of their soldiers forced the attack to halt. This was confirmed by Hitler's determination to reinforce Italy following the Allied invasion of Sicily.

Confused fighting then went on for another month, with the Germans withdrawing and the Soviets eventually recapturing Kharkov. Altogether in all this fighting, the Germans lost about half a million men, between 2,000 and 3,000 tanks and 1,400 aircraft. Although Russian losses were even larger, the USSR could absorb these, but the Reich could not. For instance, in 1943, the Soviet Union produced no less than 24,000 tanks.

Defeat at the immense Battle of Kursk heralded the eventual downfall of the German Army on the Eastern Front. They never again regained the initiative. Their long supply lines were now increasingly beset by partisan forces, which the Soviet government supported by parachuting in officers, engineers and supplies. The brilliant and trusted commanders, Zhukov and Konev, launched a series of successful offensives without any regard for the huge cost in lives. By the end of 1943, they had recaptured Kiev and crossed the Dnieper River. They were greatly helped by Hitler's incessant 'stand or die' orders, wasting his forces in fruitless resistance, often at the wrong time and place. But it was to take another eighteen months of unimaginable horror and slaughter before the war ended. The efficiency, determination and disciplined obedience of the German Army and their incessant fierce counter-attacks kept postponing their inevitable complete defeat. Most commentators would probably agree that the Wehrmacht was the outstanding land fighting force of the Second World War.

In November 1943, Churchill, Roosevelt and Stalin met in Tehran. With Churchill no longer viewed as the great pre-eminent war leader, this conference was notable for the decline of the UK/US special relationship. Their staffs were often in bitter disagreement. General Marshall and other senior American officers felt that too often they had been 'led down the garden path' by the UK. Perhaps they realised that Churchill and Brooke had sometimes been better briefed and perhaps better at arguing their case. Anyway, Roosevelt distanced himself from Churchill and gave no support to his attempts to save at least part of Poland from Soviet domination. He hoped to charm Stalin by agreeing with him on a number of issues. Together they refused to accept Churchill's hopes for further military operations to attack Germany through Southeast Europe. Instead, Operation Overlord, the cross-Channel invasion of France, was confirmed for the summer of 1944. With some difficulty, Stalin's agreement was obtained to setting up the United Nations organisation once the war was won. Much discussion was skilfully dominated by Stalin and his rigid views on the shape of post-war Europe remained unchanged. The Western leaders returned to Cairo with Churchill totally exhausted. He nearly died of pneumonia and spent weeks in Tunisia and Morocco recovering.

In the first months of 1944, the Soviet armies made further major advances from Leningrad in the north down to the Black Sea. In March, Hitler dismissed his finest commander, Field Marshal Manstein, from his command of Army Group South, and Manstein's long-lasting duel with Zuhkov was over. Together with General Brooke and General Slim, they were probably the most outstanding strategic commanders in the whole of the war. For the next year and a half, Hitler kept changing round his field marshals, who seldom lasted long enough in one command to master its complexities. Field Marshal Rundstedt was a prime victim of Hitler's capricious directives. Three times he was sacked and later reinstated in a different command before his fourth and final dismissal in 1945.

In the early summer, the Soviet High Command (the Stavka) secretly moved large forces from the southern area to face Army Group Centre, north of the Pripet Marshes. The Normandy invasion had greatly reduced the Luftwaffe's strength in the east and Soviet air supremacy allowed few reconnaissance flights. The Germans wrongly believed that the Soviet summer offensive would be in the south.

Stalin was preparing for a mighty offensive called Operation Bagration. Once again, statistics are needed to demonstrate the scale. He assembled some fifteen armies totalling nearly 1.7 million men with 6,000 self-propelled guns and tanks, supported by 7,000 aircraft, and 30,000 artillery guns stationed along a 350 mile front. The enormous onslaught started on 22 June, three years after the start of Operation Barbarossa, with some similarities but in the reverse direction.

In three weeks, Germany's Army Group Centre was largely destroyed. It was one of the most sudden and complete military disasters ever known, helped as usual by the illogical strategic concepts of Adolf Hitler. He established many towns as fortified localities from which no retreat was allowed. They were simply bypassed by the Russians and mopped up later.

The operation continued for two months, regaining Belorussia and driving the Germans back to their 1941 start line. Overall, the Wehrmacht lost many thousands of tanks and guns, and about a million men. The Red Army lost about half that number. The Russians' hatred of Germany was intensified by their finding Belorussia a virtual desert: all livestock gone, crops ploughed into the ground, a million homes burned, and most of its inhabitants dead or deported for slave labour.

In August 1944, as the Russian armies advanced into their country, the Poles in Warsaw organised an uprising to try to wrest back their city. They were heroic but ill armed. Since the Soviet Union planned to make Poland a communist state under their control, Polish nationalism did not fit this plan. And so Russian forces halted outside the city and made no attempt to intervene. Allied air drops of supplies helped the Poles a little. At one point, 2,000 men and women had to take to the sewers as a last resort. The only access was a single manhole, entered one at a time. The extraordinary queue stretched a mile and a half before they all got down. But their refuge could only be temporary. The end of the uprising was inevitable and tragic. The Waffen-SS (SS army formations) crushed the revolt with maximum ferocity, using Stuka dive-bombers, artillery and tanks; 22,000 insurgents were killed or wounded. The wounded in some Polish field hospitals were burned alive with flame throwers. About 80 per cent of Warsaw was systematically destroyed. Some reports claim that 17,000 Germans also died. Himmler's revenge was to send 154,000 men, women and children to the concentration camps, where nearly all perished. Once it was all over, the Russians resumed their control of that brave but broken country, which the United Kingdom had started the war to save.

In the late summer of 1944, the Soviet armies in the south began an advance on the Balkans. The Romanian oil fields were vital in sustaining the Wehrmacht but that country soon surrendered and then changed sides, declaring war on their erstwhile unpopular German occupiers. Advancing at speed, the Red Army reached the Yugoslavia border in one month and also threatened Budapest. Hundreds of thousands of German troops were trapped in various pockets and eventually killed or captured.

Germany was now facing serious manpower shortages. By December 1944, 2.4 million of her soldiers had died in the Soviet Union, with a much greater number wounded or captured. Russian losses were even larger but were made good from the country's vast reserves. It was probably only the terror of the NKVD following every large unit that kept Russian soldiers going while suffering such carnage.

Needed elsewhere, Germany withdrew her army from Greece, resulting in a civil war to fill the vacuum. British troops and a visit by Winston Churchill prevented a communist takeover, but the civil war dragged on for several years.

When the Red Army crossed the Danube into Bulgaria, that country, like Romania, changed sides and joined the Allies. The Russians, aided by Marshal Tito's partisan forces, then took

Belgrade. The results of Nazi barbarity, by now sickeningly familiar, greeted the liberators. They found more than 200 mass graves filled with slaughtered Slovaks. Budapest was encircled on Christmas Eve.

In the same early winter of 1944, the Baltic states of Estonia, Latvia and Lithuania were 'liberated', to remain under Stalin's iron control for the next forty-four years. Two German armies were trapped in Latvia, where Hitler had effectively created a 'fortified locality'. The Stavka treated the area as a giant prisoner of war camp maintained for them by the Wehrmacht. Its surrender was not forced until the end of the war.

Chapter 17

Invasion of France 1944

Churchill and General Brooke knew better than anyone that a large-scale amphibious landing on the heavily defended north coast of France would be a major risk. For two years, 2 million slave labourers had been constructing an 'Atlantic Wall' of fortifications along this coast. A landing could only succeed by the use of very large forces and a failure then would be a catastrophe. Churchill could not forget Gallipoli, and Brooke needed no reminding of the Dieppe disaster and the near disasters in the Torch, Salerno and Anzio landings.

A special team under Lieutenant General Sir Frederick Morgan was set up in 1942 to start the detailed planning. Normandy was chosen as the landing area. Twenty-five divisions were to land in the first month, with many more thereafter. The shipping requirement was immense. To move an armoured division across the Atlantic needed a fleet of troopships, cargo ships and escorts. Once the Battle of the Atlantic was won in May 1943, a stream of men, tanks, guns, army equipment and stores slowly turned the south of England into an enormous armed camp. The planning, which included complex shipping arrangements, was a big undertaking. The orders for a division ran to several hundred pages.

The German High Command knew in 1944 that an invasion was imminent, but where would it fall? The Allied plan included a major effort to mislead the enemy and achieve a degree of surprise. In the previous year, twice as many air operations took place over the Calais areas as over Normandy. A dummy army group 'commanded' by General Patton and visited by King George VI was invented and 'stationed' opposite Calais. It included dummy buildings, dummy tanks, and a fleet of dummy landing craft in the Thames Estuary. All of this was supported by the reports of German spies who had been 'turned' and by the appropriate volume of dummy signal traffic. There was also the sensible German belief that the Allies needed a major port to be taken in the initial assault. All this convinced Hitler that any Normandy landing would be a feint before the main invasion at Calais. This led to the stationing of hundreds of thousands of troops in Belgium, Holland and the Calais area. Hitler also insisted on keeping half a million men in Norway. He arranged a divided command in France with Rundstedt as C-in-C, Rommel commanding Army Group B for opposing the landings, and with the Panzers under a separate independent command. Finally, he unwisely insisted that the bulk of the Panzer forces stationed near Paris were not to be moved without his personal express orders.

The port problem was largely solved by a brilliant new and secret scheme. Two vast concrete floating harbours known as Mulberries were built in the West Country. These harbours weighed the same as 2,000 two-storey houses. Towed across the Channel, they would be grounded at two of the landing places.

In another engineering feat a large rubber hose was laid across the Channel seabed to pump petrol to Normandy. The code name was PLUTO (Pump Lines Under The Ocean).

Following Roosevelt and Churchill's agreement that the Supreme Commander should be an American, and with Roosevelt unable to spare his right-hand man General Marshall, they had appointed Eisenhower once again to this post. Montgomery and Air Marshal Tedder were Eisenhower's deputies. Admiral Ramsay planned and commanded the vast armada that was to cross the Channel.

It was clear that success or failure in the first few dangerous days would depend on the speed and scale of German reinforcement. If this overtook the rate of beachhead build-up, Allied forces could be thrown back into the sea. To avoid this, early in 1944 Montgomery had insisted on a big increase in the size and width of the initial landings. It was also of cardinal importance to destroy enemy road and rail communications. Air Marshal Harris was reluctant as ever to alter his main bombing strategy but was forced to do so. In the days before D-Day (the invasion date), both US and UK air forces conducted a widespread campaign to destroy railways, bridges and key road junctions across the north of France. They were assisted by the Maquis, the French resistance fighters. Churchill was deeply worried about the French civilian casualties the bombing would cause, but had to accept this. In the event, 15,000 French civilians were killed and 19,000 seriously injured. A tragedy often forgotten.

Montgomery divided his 21st Army Group into two armies for the landings. General Bradley's US First Army would assault the two western beaches codenamed Utah and Omaha at the foot of the Cherbourg Peninsula. British General Dempsey's Second Army, including Canadian 1 Corps, would land at the adjoining eastern beaches Gold, Juno and Sword. All landings would be supported by enormous air power with complete air superiority. The British 6th Airborne Division would land by parachute and glider at the eastern end of the front. They were to silence some German batteries on high ground and capture bridges over the river Orne to safeguard against a flanking counter-attack. Two US airborne divisions would land in the area behind Utah Beach. Once the beachheads were secure, General Patton's US Third Army and the Canadian First Army would pour into Normandy.

D-Day was to be 5 June, but bad weather forced Eisenhower to delay twenty-four hours. That night some thousands of ships began their slow, rough slog across the water. Their routes were cleared in advance by many squadrons of minesweepers. They carried the hopes and fears of 150,000 US, British and Canadian soldiers who all knew that many would die. Senior leaders at home who bore the ultimate responsibility for success or catastrophic failure held their breath. Many prayers were said. This greatest amphibious landing in history was supported by five battleships, twenty-three cruisers, and 117 destroyers and frigates, plus 118 destroyers and other warships in reserve. On the first day, 154,000 troops landed, supported by 13,000 aircraft sorties.

The landings on the whole went well, with the exception of Omaha. This curving beach was geographically easy to defend. Gun positions on high cliffs and heavy machine-gun posts on the wings poured intensive fire on the heavily weighted US soldiers stumbling in the shallows from their landing craft. Many Sherman tanks failed to get ashore in the rough sea, landing craft capsized, and many men, particularly the wounded, were drowned. With 2,000 of his soldiers killed, General Bradley considered calling off the whole operation. But eventually, after heroic efforts, supported by heavy naval gunfire support, the cliffs were scaled and the tide began to turn. By nightfall, 34,000 men had got ashore and the beachhead was becoming secure.

Montgomery planned to take Caen in the first day or two. But unknown to Allied intelligence, the 21st Panzer Division, with its Tiger tanks and fearsome 88 millimetre anti-tank guns, was already in the Caen area. The narrow sunken roads and thick hedges made the countryside easy to defend. All the Second Army attacks were repulsed with heavy tank losses. Progress became even more difficult with the arrival of a new SS division. They fought fanatically and shot any of our men who surrendered. Allied soldiers soon followed suit. The situation worsened as a storm at sea wrecked one of the two Mulberries and delayed the build-up. Also, low cloud frequently reduced air operations.

The US Army further to the west faced less concentrated forces but still had to fight hard to make progress. They were hampered by flooded marshland at the foot of the Cherbourg Peninsula, where many of their paratroopers had drowned. Nevertheless, after intensive fighting they captured Cherbourg at the end of June. It then took six weeks to clear the German damage before the port became usable.

As the stalemate around Caen continued, with each new offensive failing, it was important that there were still half a million German troops guarding the Calais area against an invasion that would never come. It was also important that further Panzer reinforcements were successfully delayed. Meanwhile, Montgomery himself came under widespread criticism. There was even talk of a replacement.

The SS Das Reich Panzer Division in the south of France set out on 8 June to reinforce Normandy. This was a 450 mile journey, which they could expect to complete in a few days. But the road and rail bombing and heroic guerrilla operations by the French Maquis extended the journey to three weeks. The Maquis were much assisted by the combined UK/US Operation Jedburgh. This involved parachuting in many very small teams of highly trained soldiers to provide advice and leadership, as well as arms and ammunition. In retaliation for the delays, the SS division took fearful reprisals. The most infamous was at the small village of Oradour, where they murdered the entire population of 642 people, including 190 school children. The men were shot, the women and children burnt alive in a barn, and the village was completely razed. While this was an exceptionally dreadful act in the war in the west, it has been pointed out that it was little different from the German Army's behaviour in Russia since 1941.

The extent to which other German generals knew about and collaborated in many such war crimes was revealed about this time. Captured German generals and senior officers were interned in the UK at a centre called Trent Park. They were encouraged to discuss the war between themselves, little knowing that their communal rooms were bugged and every word recorded by stenographers and interpreters. The truth about the murder of Jews, Russians, Poles and the mentally or physically disabled was common currency in their 'private' conversations. A few, at least, expressed horror. But the records comprehensively explode post-war claims that they had no knowledge of these crimes and that only SS units were to blame.

It is perhaps surprising that these civilised men, with their proud military traditions, were party to so many war crimes. One might guess that it was primarily because of their rigid code of obedience plus professional ambition. Military tradition always required the army to see themselves as the servants of the civilian government. Whatever the reasons, they could and should have done better. Senior officers who stood up to Hitler and even disobeyed him were not generally ill-treated. Normally they just missed out on financial reward, were retired or were moved to another post. In the same way, no person, as far as we know, was ever shot for refusing to murder Jews.

It is only fair to say that Allied forces committed war crimes too, including shooting enemy soldiers who had surrendered. But this was rarely in cold blood and usually in direct retaliation to enemy behaviour. In any case, the scale of such crime was so small as to bear no comparison with German or Japanese atrocities, or indeed those perpetrated by the Red Army.

July saw two developments of importance. First there was Colonel von Stauffenberg's unsuccessful attempt to assassinate Hitler, organised by about twenty army officers. This has been dramatised in the film *Valkyrie*. Hitler was lucky to escape with only light wounds when the bomb went off at his headquarters. Only about a hundred people were directly implicated in the plot but the Gestapo made mass arrests and eventually about 11,000 were executed. Field Marshal Rommel was not a conspirator but the Gestapo rightly believed he was a sympathiser. Facing arrest, he shot himself at his home. Field Marshal von Kluge, at one time C-in-C West, also committed suicide in similar circumstances. There were few generals Hitler ever really trusted again.

Then, at the end of June, Germany launched a new air offensive against the UK with the V-1 flying bomb. This was a crude type of pilotless drone, containing nearly a ton of high explosive, launched from Europe's north coast, with an approximate maximum range of 130 miles. When it reached the range set, it dived to earth and exploded. If one heard the 'doodlebug' passing overhead, one's safety was assured. But hearing the engine stop meant that an explosion was sure to be close. To help protect London, British intelligence agencies running ex-German spies who had been 'turned', sent false messages back to Berlin reporting V-1s landing just north of London. This sometimes encouraged the Germans to reduce the set range, which may have been bad luck for Kent but provided some open countryside for the flying bombs to fall in. Many were shot down, but something like 10,000 landed in or near London, killing about 6,000 people before the launch sites were overrun in March 1945.

The V-1 was followed in September by the V-2 rocket, a 13 ton ballistic missile that descended on London with no warning from a height of over 50 miles. There was no defence, and the 1 ton warhead, which could penetrate deep shelters, caused immense damage. Four of them landed in Croydon in one day and destroyed or badly damaged 1,000 houses. The V-2 was hugely expensive and used large amounts of Germany's scarce material resources. It is also estimated that up to 15,000 slave labourers died during its underground production. Over five months, some 3,000 were launched, killing about 9,000 British civilians and injuring at least twice that number. But neither the V-1 bomb nor V-2 rocket were in any way the decisive weapons that Hitler intended. They were too late and too few. If Hitler had started their development a year or two earlier with greater priority and much greater numbers, the story might be different. But in those years, German industry was desperately producing tanks, planes and guns to try to keep the Russians at bay, and could spare limited effort to produce 'vengeance weapons'. After the war, the V-2's chief designer, Wernher von Braun, and many of his team, were employed in America to help design the rockets used for space exploration.

On 25 July, General Bradley launched a new offensive to encircle the German forces in Normandy. Despite some of the US Air Force support bombing falling short and killing 500 American soldiers, the operation was quickly successful. The Americans took the important town of Saint-Lô. General Patton, now leading the US Third Army, moved on at blitzkrieg speed. He had encouraged his soldiers with the exhortation 'No bastard ever won a war by dying for his country. You win the war by making the other poor dumb bastard die for his country.'

The other arm of the pincer would be provided by British and Canadian forces attacking south from Caen. The Germans in Normandy were soon surrounded except for a small area called the Falaise Gap, through which about 20,000 escaped. The rest were now attacked from all sides and the carnage was terrible. The main bulk of the German Seventh Army, Fifth Panzer Army and a separate Panzer group were killed or captured together with their equipment. It was an enormous victory.

Montgomery afterwards claimed that it had always been his plan for the British and Canadian armies to keep the bulk of the German forces occupied at Caen. This would be the hinge for the wide sweep of the US armies to encircle them. But historians have also claimed that he had the unusual gift of combining very bold speech and very cautious action. Nevertheless, as the overall Army Commander it is to his credit that the Normandy landings and build-up were so successful and casualties less than feared. It may also be relevant that many Allied soldiers this late in the war were understandably more interested in self-preservation than in adopting a forceful offensive spirit. Apart from some elite forces such as Paratroops or US Rangers, most of the men on the Allied side were quickly trained conscripted civilians. It is not surprising if some failed to match the fervour of those indoctrinated from early youth into the Nazi warrior mindset.

General de Gaulle's Free French forces hurried on and triumphantly entered Paris against little opposition. Thankfully the German commander had refused to carry out Hitler's order to destroy the city.

From D-Day on 6 June to 21 August, the Allies landed over 2 million men in France. Canada lost 5,000 killed, the Second British Army containing many nationalities lost 11,000 killed, and the US armies 20,600. Many more of course were wounded or captured. Allied air forces flew over 480,000 sorties, losing 4,100 aircraft. America and Britain shared equally in the 16,000 aircrew lost. They also lost about 4,000 tanks. Estimates of German losses in the campaign vary widely. They must have numbered several hundred thousand men and about 2,000 tanks. Lots of statistics again and there will be more to come. But we should remember that they do not record, in scenes of hell, the awful agonies, prayers and screams of the wounded and dying.

Shellshock, or more accurately psychological combat exhaustion, was prevalent in the Allied armies. In the German Army, perhaps because of their longer training and experience, it was less so. In any case, they simply treated it as cowardice. But the Allies understood the realities and accepted it. In the campaign in France, some

30,000 men in the US First Army were accounted cases of psycho-neurotic breakdown. Figures for other armies are not available but are, one supposes, likely to be similar.

As Allied troops rushed eastwards across France, initially against little opposition, Eisenhower took over command of all ground forces from Montgomery, to the latter's intense chagrin. He was left with command of the 21st Army Group and encouraged by promotion to the rank of field marshal. Eisenhower's plan was for a broad advance into Germany. Montgomery had argued for a narrow thrust into the Ruhr industrial area spearheaded by his army group. Patton, whose military achievements were as immense as his lack of modesty and dislike of Montgomery, had another plan, to be led by his Third US Army in the south. General Omar Bradley felt that the central drive of his Twelfth US Army Group on Frankfurt should have priority. Sometimes it seemed that the generals' own egos dictated their strategic choice. Or perhaps it was their proper confidence in their undoubted ability and the prowess of their soldiers. Either way, Eisenhower's greatness stems partly from his success in controlling these very strong individuals and holding the ring.

In September, the Guards Armoured Division entered Brussels in scenes of wild excitement. Antwerp fell to the US Eleventh Armoured Division, which had advanced 340 miles in six days. It was the important strategic key to solving the acute supply problems of the Allied armies. However, it could not be used while the approaches up the Scheldt Estuary from the open sea some 50 miles away were still in German hands. Astonishingly, neither Eisenhower nor Montgomery seemed to realise the urgent importance of clearing these approaches while thinly held by German forces still in disarray. Once they were reinforced by the Germans they became a real problem. Clearing the estuary and Walcheren Island eventually took the Canadian First Army and four British divisions the best part of two months, fighting in difficult bitter winter conditions. The task should have been done in September at much less cost. This delay must be seen as a serious strategic failure, which probably prolonged the war. Military historians put most of the blame on Montgomery.

The first supply ship docked in Antwerp on 28 November. Until then, as the Channel ports were still in German hands, all supplies had to continue coming hundreds of miles from Cherbourg and Normandy. At this time, General Patton was nearing the Rhine but the lack of petrol stalled all major advances. Meanwhile, large German reinforcements came forward to defend their homeland. US forces were also reinforced by another American army, which had advanced from its landing in the South of France but also added to the supply problems.

Montgomery was frustrated by Eisenhower's strategy and their mistrust was mutual. However, Monty (as he was popularly known) somehow persuaded him to agree to a highly ambitious operation called Market Garden. The aim was to facilitate General Montgomery's long held wish for a major thrust to encircle the Ruhr from the north. The plan was for the 1st British Airborne Division to capture the bridge over the Rhine at Arnhem in the Netherlands, some 60 miles behind the German front line. At the same time, the 82nd and 101st US Airborne divisions would be dropped to capture intervening bridges at Eindhoven, Grave, and Nijmegen. Without heavy weapons or transport, airborne forces could not expect to occupy and hold their area against tanks and artillery for more than a short period. Success therefore depended on the British XXX Corps being able to fight their way with tanks quickly up the long single road to support and relieve the airborne troops. Americans and some senior British commanders were astonished that the usually cautious Montgomery was launching such an ambitious operation. It completely underestimated the difficulties of XXX Corps' task and the furious energy of German reaction. Also, no account was taken of the remains of two SS Panzer divisions known to be refitting in the Arnhem area.

On 17 September, the US airborne divisions were dropped at Eindhoven and Nijmegen, and the British at Arnhem. But despite heroic bravery by all the formations, the operation sadly failed. Things went wrong from the beginning. Bad weather prevented air support. The British drop, which included a Polish brigade, landed too far (6 miles) from Arnhem and with almost complete inter-unit communication failures, lost all surprise. The US forces reached and held some of their target bridges but only one British battalion reached Arnhem itself. After four days, with half their number killed or wounded, and supplies exhausted, they were overwhelmed by superior German forces. The armoured divisions under General Horrocks reached

Eindhoven and Nijmegen by 19 September but could not battle their way through in time to come to the aid of the British 1st Division. They were subsequently criticised for a lack of urgency and failure to take risks in the interest of speed. And so the Paras' heroic fight in Arnhem finished when, with water, rations and ammunition expended, 1,741 of the battered remnants of the division were evacuated by night across the Rhine. The rest were killed or captured. The Americans lost 4,000 dead, wounded or captured, the British and Poles at least twice as many. It was a thoroughly bad plan, never likely to succeed, and Montgomery's reputation was damaged. Lieutenant General 'Boy' Browning, the commander in charge of the landings, was somewhat surprisingly knighted. Dutch civilians, who welcomed Allied troops, suffered about 3,600 killed, 180,000 forced from their homes, and 20,000 starved following German reprisals.

In October, Churchill had another meeting with Stalin in Moscow. To his great credit he was passionate in his hope to save some independence for Poland, even if it meant new borders. But when he mentioned Poland's essential Catholicism and the importance of relations with the Vatican, the unmoved Stalin made his famous contemptuous reply: 'How many divisions does the Pope have?' Later in the discussion Churchill produced a list of Eastern European countries with in each case a suggested division of influence between the Soviet Union and the West. Mostly it accepted Soviet domination, except for Greece, where it was proposed to score only 10 per cent. With only minor amendment, Stalin agreed to this sudden unorthodox proposal. This was important in that in later upheavals in Greece, Stalin gave no significant support to the Communist party trying to gain control of that country.

Meanwhile on the borders of the Reich, strong German counter-attacks held up any general advance, although Allied forces had some success. The US First Army, after heavy fighting, took Aachen, the first German city to fall. Patton's Third Army was attacking Metz. Further south, Free French forces eventually took Strasbourg.

One rather sad operation may be worth a brief account because it to some extent illustrates the horror of the war. North of the Ardennes, the US First Army, in constant rain and sleet, started a large infantry assault through the Hürtgen Forest. The dark concentration of pine trees, stretching for many miles, was easily defended by large German forces. They had built well camouflaged earth bunkers, and spread thousands of anti-personnel mines and booby traps. The US Infantry had suffered heavy losses since D-Day, and an increasing proportion were barely trained and very inexperienced. They were quite unused to being without their normal supporting tanks, often lost their way, and feared the baleful hostile darkness. Attack after attack failed and casualties mounted. The soldiers lacked foul weather clothing in the non-stop awful weather. Many suffered crippling trench foot and dysentery. There was a dramatic rise in panicking retreats, desertions and suicides. Division after division failed and was pulled out of the line. The American soldiers suffered psychological and physical exhaustion and 33,000 casualties, before the operation was called off.

In these years, almost all Allied operations continued to be greatly helped by Bletchley Park. Deciphering German signal traffic provided fairly regular intelligence on German strengths, weaknesses and intentions. But now, on one important occasion, this intelligence was denied. In the stalemate autumn of 1944, Hitler was developing plans for a massive offensive designed to break through Allied lines, reach the Meuse, and then wheel right to reach the Channel. The utmost secrecy was observed. Telephones were used and no mention was allowed on radio traffic. He hoped it would encircle Allied forces in the north and inflict a major defeat – perhaps even achieve a separate peace and save much of Germany. Field Marshal Rundstedt and other senior generals regarded the plan as so hopelessly optimistic as to be suicidal. Their advice, as usual, was ignored.

Five Panzer divisions and twelve mechanised infantry divisions were assembled in great secrecy in the Ardennes and Eifel forests. Continual bad weather prevented any aerial observation. Eisenhower, together with General Bradley, whose army group was spread north and south of the Ardennes, thought any attack through the 80 mile front of the forest was most unlikely. It was therefore covered thinly with just six divisions.

Suddenly, on 16 December, three German armies comprising 200,000 men came crashing out of the forests with their Tiger tanks. Some US divisions with inexperienced units or those recuperating from earlier battles were quickly broken. Others fought hard and slowed the advance. There was much confusion at

Allied headquarters as the tanks roared on and rapidly established a deep protrusion. This led to its name, the Battle of the Bulge, which eventually extended 50 miles deep and 40 miles wide.

But General Eisenhower acted calmly and firmly. Some think it was his finest hour. He decided to give command of Bradley's US First and Ninth armies in the north to Montgomery with the 21st Army Group. This left Bradley with his one army to the south of the Bulge and he was deeply unhappy. Other American commanders were also appalled, but Eisenhower sensibly held fast. General Montgomery found some confusion in the US First Army, not well placed under its indecisive leader General Hodges. Monty quickly sorted things out and positioned his armies to stabilise the situation and prepare to counter-attack. But in this process he failed to understand or credit the extraordinary resilience of many American units.

The US 101st Airborne Division arrived at the town of Bastogne on 20 December, just hours before the Panzer division reached its vital crossroads. The Americans were quickly surrounded. In freezing weather, supply problems had left them still in summer uniforms. Dreadfully cold, they held the town against the odds with tigerish determination, but suffered horribly. Standing in their foxholes in icy, slushy mud, they suffered from dysentery and trench foot, which accounted for a large proportion of their casualties. Nevertheless, when invited to surrender, their commander answered with the single word 'Nuts'. It was to become a famous reply.

Patton's US Third Army, with great skill and their usual dash, turned to attack the Bulge from the south. They fought through and relieved the gallant Bastogne defenders on Boxing Day.

The 6th SS Panzer Division led the northern arm of the attack, also with skill and great determination. But low on fuel, they eventually met equally determined and well led American forces and were halted just short of the 4 million gallon fuel dumps near Stavelot. Their savage exploits included killing about a hundred unarmed American prisoners in cold blood. It is not surprising that, in angry reprisals, many Germans were shot rather than taken prisoner.

By the end of the month the leading Panzers approaching the Meuse were running out of fuel. Moreover, as the weather improved, they had to cope with a tremendous air onslaught, making daylight movement almost impossible. The Luftwaffe gathered 800 fighters in a desperate attempt to take out Allied airfields. About a hundred of them were shot down by their own poorly briefed AA batteries. Overall their losses were very heavy and Allied aircraft regained complete command. Under sustained American pressure the great offensive started to peter out. At the end of January, the Germans started a general retreat. The American forces had inflicted on them a major defeat. The battle cost the Germans 98,000 casualties, plus the loss of 700 tanks and 1,600 aircraft. Figures for American losses were not much different. But they could make up the losses, whilst Germany could not.

In London, General Brooke, who knew Montgomery's good and bad qualities very well, worried about what he would say at a press conference after the battle. His worry was justified. Apart from paying brief tribute to the American soldiers' courage, Montgomery was boastful, inept, and completely lacking tact. He implied that he and his armies had come to the rescue and saved the poor US forces from defeat. Whilst his forces had played an important part, this was a totally false picture. The resentment of the Americans, who had done most of the fighting, was deep and widespread. In particular, Bradley and Patton were extremely angry and could never thereafter trust or cooperate with the now hated field marshal.

Montgomery then wrote an arrogant letter to his boss Eisenhower. The latter, already angry, was now quite furious. He drafted a signal to the Joint Chiefs of Staff demanding Montgomery's replacement or he himself would resign. Montgomery's brilliant and much liked Chief of Staff, Major General de Guingand, heard about this and persuaded Eisenhower to hold the draft for twenty-four hours. He then got his master to write an abject apology and things reverted to their normal unhappy state.

Montgomery was now a British hero. With the exception of Field Marshal Brooke, despite Arnhem and Antwerp, he was the most able general available. The only possible successor was the elegant and charming General Alexander, the Mediterranean overall commander, but Brooke had a low opinion of him. It was therefore considered vital that Montgomery should keep his job. Eisenhower was perhaps the only man with the diplomatic skills to make this possible.

Chapter 18

The Far East 1944 and 1945

In January 1944, XV Corps, part of General Slim's Fourteenth Army, fought an important battle in Arakan, a region in north-west Burma. They formed a number of fortified 'boxes' deep in the jungle, a new tactic allowing for Japanese encirclement. Spitfires and Hurricanes drove the Japanese fighters from the sky and air drops supplied those encircled. In three weeks of fighting none of the XV Corps positions were captured and none attempted retreat. Thirty-thousand Japanese troops were completely defeated and withdrew. Because of a threat to its rear, XV Corps also then had to withdraw. But the legend of Japanese invincibility in the jungle was smashed. A triumph for the Fourteenth Army and General Slim's punishing training regime and new tactics.

With the personal enthusiastic support of Churchill, the Chindit operations had grown in size, and the British, Indian and Gurkha troops involved had gone through a comprehensive and rigorous training. In March 1944, three brigades each of 3,000 men, accompanied by 1,000 mules and supplied by air drops, were fighting behind enemy lines. Many of these gallant men became emaciated and exhausted as they tried to cope with leeches, lice, malaria, hunger and forced marches through the sodden jungle.

Some just died in their sleep. Without doubt they tied down large numbers of enemy troops and were at least a major nuisance. They also assisted General Stilwell with his Chinese army in the capture of Myitkyina, an important strategic air base in north-east Burma. Certainly their operations are considered by many to be one of the greatest military feats of the war. But as with most special forces, it is difficult to assess their true value. General Slim provided Wingate with much support but had difficulties controlling his wildest excesses and furious demands. Sadly, in March 1944, Orde Wingate, then a major general, was killed in an air crash.

Burma Command was now preparing to defend against a Japanese offensive into India, threatened by the Japanese Fifteenth Army of 156,000 men. However, the size and speed of the enemy advance was underestimated and British forces were ill placed to counter it. For their success both sides needed large supplies of food, ammunition and military equipment. The Japanese target was the vast British supply dump measuring 11 square miles inside the Indian border at Dimapur. About 100 miles to the south, the town of Imphal had another supply. The key to both, on the only road between them, was the small Indian village hill station at Kohima.

Early in April, while one Japanese division started a battle at Imphal, 6,000 of their troops cut the road and besieged Kohima. This was defended by only about 1,000 soldiers including a battalion of the Royal West Kent Regiment plus a few hundred locally raised Indian troops. The fighting there is described by one writer 'as desperate as any in recorded history'. For a fortnight the Japanese bombarded by day and then launched wave after wave of infantry attacks at night. Their casualties were heavy and dead bodies littered the barbed wire surrounds. But gradually more buildings were captured in vicious hand-to-hand fighting. There was much heroism on both sides, sometimes only the width of a tennis court apart. After two weeks, one third of the defenders were casualties. The bedraggled and filthy remainder became increasingly exhausted as their numbers dwindled and the dead and wounded lay around them, unmoved where they fell. By late April, however, relieving troops had forced their way through, and the battle widened with fresh Allied forces.

Two posthumous Victoria Crosses were awarded. The first was won by Lance Corporal John Harman of the Royal West Kents. In a dire situation he single-handedly charged and took out two machine-gun posts in succession before being shot. The other went to Captain Jack Randle, who had just taken over command of a Norfolk Regiment company after its commander was killed during an attack. His soldiers came under heavy machine-gun fire from a Japanese bunker and the attack was in danger of failing. Already wounded, he charged the bunker on his own, and although wounded once again, he just managed to throw a grenade through the bunker slit. Before dying, he flung his body against the slit to make it completely sealed. His action led to an important victory and was typical of many such magnificent acts of bravery during the war.

The memorial in the Kohima cemetery is believed to be the first to bear the famous moving lines:

When you go home
Tell them of us and say
For your tomorrow
We gave our today

Whilst Allied forces had complete air superiority and could supply jungle troops by air, Japan was fighting at the end of long and difficult supply lines often cut by the Chindits and with almost no air support. Little food got through. The Japanese were slowly driven back out of their massive dugouts, starving and exhausted. Their failure to capture Imphal or Kohima was critical. Harried also by Stillwell's Chinese forces, as the monsoon arrived in May, their offensive petered out in retreat. They had lost 55,000 men, half of this number by starvation and disease. It was the biggest defeat in Japanese history and it saved India. It also did much for the morale of the Fourteenth Army, whose exhausted soldiers stuck in trenches in the jungle, drenched by the monsoon, plagued by vicious insects, beset by malaria and other unpleasant tropical diseases, faced a barbaric enemy. As evidence of their courage, the Gurkhas were awarded eight Victoria Crosses in 1944. They were the bravest of the brave. Army casualties in the victories in Arakan, Kohima, Imphal and behind enemy lines amounted to 10,000 dead, 2,000 missing and 27,000 wounded. But together with the operations of General Stilwell's Chinese, they had virtually destroyed five Japanese divisions and severely degraded the Imperial Japanese Army's ability to defend Burma.

In China, the Japanese were more successful in the 'Ichi-Go' offensive against the nationalist army – to the great satisfaction of Mao Zedong and his Chinese communist forces. This success forced the United States to demolish and abandon thirteen of its air bases in that country. By the end of the year, President Chiang Kai-shek's armies were utterly defeated having suffered 300,000 casualties. The abrasive General Stilwell quarrelled with the Chinese president and was eventually recalled to a new post at home.

But this was to no avail to Japan in the Pacific War. Here the US Navy and Marines continued their valiant fighting to recapture island chains taken by Japan. The Japanese soldiers always fought to the death and the Marines suffered heavy casualties. However, with the navy's command of the sea, they could sometimes bypass individual strongly held islands, and by preventing any resupply, leave their defenders to starve.

One important island chain was the Marianas. In 1944 it was decided to retake these islands to provide airfields suitable as bases from which B29 Superfortresses could bomb Japan. On 15 June, an invasion force supported by Admiral Spruance's enormous fleet of 535 warships landed 20,000 Marines on the largest island, Saipan. They faced 32,000 defenders in well-constructed positions and a violent battle commenced. An American submarine then detected the Japanese fleet, which included nine carriers, approaching from 180 miles away. Spruance sent a task force with fifteen carriers to intercept. Their Hellcat fighter aircraft were superior to the Japanese Zeros and over several days shot down about 400 enemy aircraft. US dive and torpedo bombers sank one carrier and US submarines accounted for another two. American losses were very small.

The same could not be said for the brave soldiers on Saipan. When the Japanese were finally defeated they left the corpses of 30,000 men on the battlefield. The US Marines lost 14,000 killed or wounded; 7,000 Japanese civilians also died, mostly by suicide, jumping off the cliffs into the sea. The other islands were then soon taken and the airfields extended to take the B29 heavy bombers.

As the year went on, General MacArthur's army had much success in New Guinea and nearby islands. The Japanese were forced to abandon their large air and naval base at Rabaul. MacArthur now persuaded Roosevelt to order a new offensive, with the full support of the US fleet, to recapture the Philippines. And so, in October 1944, the US Sixth Army was transported to that island archipelago, protected by the US fleet. Some 130,000 troops were put ashore in one day on the island of Leyte to start a long and bloody battle. This redeemed General MacArthur's famous promise to the Philippine people, 'I shall return.' The General organised a big PR operation to make sure this was widely featured.

The Japanese High Command were expecting this invasion and assembled their combined fleets to take on the Americans. They had a cunning plan to decoy the largest fleet away to the north while they launched an attack with most of their ships on the smaller forces supporting the landing. In a sort of stately nautical game of hide and seek over three days it nearly worked, but eventually a major encounter took place. It was known as the Battle of Leyte Gulf and became the biggest naval engagement ever recorded. Although serious mistakes were made by both sides, it ended in a huge American victory. The Japanese lost four aircraft carriers, three battleships, and ten cruisers. They sank only one US light aircraft carrier, two escort carriers and two destroyers. The US Pacific Fleet was now a huge force. By the end of 1944, they had a hundred aircraft carriers at sea.

The battles in the Philippines went on until the end of the war as the Japanese stubbornly fought to save the island of Luzon and the capital Manila. MacArthur's army at one stage made fourteen major landings in just six weeks. On one island they discovered the charred remains of 150 US prisoners of war who had been soaked in petrol and set alight by their guards. Another tragedy was on a larger scale. Very large numbers of civilians got trapped in the fierce fighting round Manila; 100,000 are said to have died.

In Burma in December 1944, the engineers installed a 380-yard bridge across the Chindwin River, and XXXV Corps and IV Corps of the no longer 'Forgotten' Fourteenth Army started their next great task. This was to reopen the Burma Road, fight their way 300 miles south to retake the city of Mandalay, and then fight on to Rangoon to expel the hated Japanese from the whole country.

Supply problems were immense and some ingenious makeshifts helped to solve them. A company of elephants was formed to help build bridges, improve cart tracks, and haul trees to build rafts. These could carry a tank or 10 tons of stores downriver. But overall the difficulties of long-distance supply could only be surmounted by a constant flow of air drops. These were superbly organised and carried out by the RAF, often in very dangerous flying weather. General Slim suggested to his brilliant supply chief, Alf Snelling, that he include a case of rum in every fifth consignment to encourage men to search for loads dropped off target. Slim said he got back a pitying look and the reply that a case of rum had already been ordered for every consignment. The Royal Navy also helped by ferrying stores and men along the coast.

When the Japanese General Kimura withdrew his army across the mighty, wide Irrawaddy River to a defensive position on the bank, Slim faced a problem. A frontal assault would incur very heavy losses. He decided on an outflanking movement, accepting the serious risks involved. General Messervy with his IV Corps was sent on a clandestine 300-mile march far to the west, eventually to threaten the enemy's rear. Far from any support, if discovered they faced possible annihilation. But the bold and brilliant plan worked. General Kimura, fearful of being surrounded, withdrew to the south. Men, mules, guns, tanks and supplies of both corps, some 200 miles apart, poured across the Irrawaddy. Their long advance had been exhausting but their courage and confident fighting spirit had made them unstoppable. Brilliant tactics led to the fall of

Mandalay after a tough battle with many casualties. The Japanese Army was then effectively wrecked in ferocious close-quarter combat at the Battle of Meiktila. Eventually, as the monsoon broke in May, Rangoon was reached. To escape a threatened amphibious assault, the Japanese remnants withdrew into Thailand. After three years, Burma was now recovered.

In a rare error of judgement, Churchill gave the credit for this great victory to Mountbatten and the C-in-C General Leese, and bizarrely to Wingate. Of course, Admiral Mountbatten and Leese had great responsibilities, but their role in Burma was primarily to approve Slim's plans and provide support and background organisation to meet his priorities. With his brilliant generalship and exceptional leadership the victory belonged in truth to Slim, later Lieutenant General Sir William Slim KCB DSO MC.

After the victory, in a less well-known event, General Leese amazingly informed Slim that he was relieving him of command of the Fourteenth Army on the grounds of tiredness and unsuitability to plan and conduct the next big offensive in Malaysia. Instead he should remain in Burma to oversee the army's policing of that country as it tried to return to normality. It was a quite amazing decision, which appalled all who soon got to know. Leese had discussed it with Mountbatten, but the latter later denied that he had given his approval. Slim accepted that the C-in-C had a right to make the decision and accepted it calmly without protest. However, he declined to accept the lesser post under a C-in-C who had no trust in him. Instead he would quietly retire. A storm of protest was now beginning to arise, with talk of resignations and even mutinies. When the news reached the Chiefs of Staff, the chairman, General Brooke, was furious. After consulting the Supreme Commander Mountbatten, he ordered a reversal with Slim to take over as C-in-C from Leese, and the latter to return home and the lesser post of Commander UK Eastern Command.

After the war Bill Slim eventually became a field marshal with the top army post, Chief of the Imperial General Staff. Subsequently he was an exceptionally popular Governor General of Australia. On retirement he was deservedly awarded a peerage. He is featured in these pages because many believe he was one of the finest British generals in history.

Earlier in 1944 a serious argument developed between Churchill and the Chiefs of Staff. Churchill believed strongly in deploying a fleet in the Indian Ocean to help in the reconquest of British imperial possessions. Brooke and his fellow Chiefs took a different and seemingly political view. They believed it would be right and fitting for the navy to operate with Australian forces alongside the Americans in the final stages of the war. This was eventually accepted and the British Pacific Fleet deployed accordingly. It included four aircraft carriers and two battleships, much less than half the size of the US fleet commanded by Admiral Nimitz, but still significant. However, the Royal Navy was regrettably shown to be years behind the US Navy in its ability to replenish at sea, its propulsive machinery, anti-aircraft gunnery, and very inferior carrier aircraft. Some see the latter as the legacy of the earlier management by the Royal Air Force, together with a lack of funds and the incompetence of some British aircraft firms. But it is difficult to see how the Admiralty can escape blame for many of the deficiencies. In contrast, the seamanship and fighting spirit of the Royal Navy's men had never been higher. Awoken from the conservatism and complacency of the inter-war years, it was a bold, resourceful, and, as far as its equipment allowed, highly professional Service.

Meanwhile, things continued to go badly for Japan. Heavy bombing raids hammered their cities. In March 1945, 350 US bombers with incendiaries reduced large areas of Tokyo to ashes and killed about 85,000 people. In the continuing island hopping campaign, Japan incurred further widespread naval losses.

The small island of Iwo Jima, about 800 miles from Japan, was strategically important because its airfield could support the American bombing campaign by providing a landing haven for damaged aircraft. In February 1945, 30,000 US Marines were landed to take on the 21,000 defenders. The latter were organised in a very strong defensive maze of fortified caves and tunnels. As usual, they fought to the death. When the Marines made it to the top of a dormant volcano, they were photographed raising the Stars and Stripes on a long metal pole. The photo has remained famous as an icon of the Pacific War. The US Secretary of the Navy, James Forrestal, who was observing the operation, remarked that the flag raising would ensure the future of the US Marine Corps for another 500 years. Their level of courage and commitment can be judged by the fact that twenty-seven won Medals of Honor, a high award. At the end in March, the United States had about 200 prisoners. The rest of the 21,000 defenders were all dead. The Americans had 25,000 killed or seriously wounded.

One of the effects of the war in the Far East was the dislocation of normal trade. This was accentuated by Japanese destruction of farming, and seizure or sinking of shipping. The resultant famine in Indo-China killed more than 2 million people.

In October 1944, Japan had started using a deadly new form of suicidal air attack – the kamikaze. This involved volunteer pilots intentionally crashing their bomb-laden aircraft into Allied warships. Although only about one fifth of attacks were successful, altogether they sank thirty-four ships and damaged hundreds. US aircraft carriers with their wooden decks were very vulnerable. The British carriers had armoured decks and suffered much less from these attacks. Four thousand kamikaze pilots lost their lives. They played an important part in the battle for Okinawa.

In the spring of 1945, the Americans decided it was important to capture another island, called Okinawa. Sixty miles long by 8 miles wide, it was dominated by a series of limestone hills, and had a population of about 500,000. With its airfields only 350 miles from Japan, it was considered a vital springboard for the intended invasion of the mainland. The Japanese were determined to defend it as if part of their homeland. Over the months, they had tunnelled under the hills to create a vast underground fortress to house

135,000 defenders together with all their supplies and weapons. Innumerable hidden openings provided artillery and machine-gun positions, invisible from the air and easily closed in defence.

On 1 April, after a huge but largely ineffective naval bombardment lasting several days, the first units of the 280,000-strong US Tenth Army landed virtually unopposed. But once they reached the southern hills the ferocious fighting began. It went on for nearly three months. The US Marines and infantry, often soaked in their foxholes in heavy rain, with much use of flamethrowers and grenades, slowly overwhelmed the defences thought to be impregnable. Corporal Desmond Doss was a conscientious objector serving as a combat medic. He was awarded the Medal of Honor for gallantry in a series of extremely brave actions in saving his comrades' lives. These included carrying seventy-five wounded men individually from a fire-swept area. This became the subject of a film called *Hacksaw Ridge*.

The supporting naval forces suffered heavily from a total of 1,465 kamikaze attacks: thirty ships were sunk and 120 damaged. The Japanese 72,000 ton battleship *Yamato*, with her 18-inch guns the heaviest warship ever built, was sent towards the area with only enough fuel for a one-way trip. A sort of naval kamikaze. Three hundred US carrier aircraft, in a succession of attacks, eventually sank her together with her crew of 2,500 men.

As their last command post on Okinawa fell, the Japanese commander Lieutenant General Ushijima and his chief of staff committed the ritual disembowelling of hara-kiri. The gruesome ceremony included their decapitation at the same time by their personal guards. Approximately 120,000 Japanese soldiers and up to 100,000 civilians died in this terrible land and sea battle. Ashore and afloat, America had 12,000 killed, 32,000 wounded, plus about 20,000 who suffered psychological breakdown. The casualties included Lieutenant General Buckner, the highest ranking Allied officer to be killed in action in the war. The United States also lost 763 aircraft, the Japanese an amazing 2,800.

In the battle for Okinawa the British fleet played a useful but comparatively small part. One of the destroyer officers involved was Lieutenant Philip Mountbatten, later Duke of Edinburgh. In another comparatively minor operation late in the war, five British destroyers sank the Japanese cruiser *Haguro* in a classic torpedo attack.

Despite the heavy toll of Okinawa, Japan fought on in Luzon and Borneo. One historian observed that the Japanese soldier might be a subhuman creature who tortured and starved those he captured, but there was never a braver soldier. It is estimated that more than half the 1.74 million who perished actually died from disease or starvation. No wonder there were many occasions when they resorted to cannibalism.

President Franklin Delano Roosevelt died in April 1945 and Harry S. Truman took over as the new president and C-in-C. He and General Marshall faced a difficult situation. Whilst Japan was now effectively defeated, her leaders showed no signs of surrendering. It was clear that an invasion of the mainland would be resisted with the same fanatical determination already shown. When defending their own sacred soil, their determination to die rather than surrender might perhaps be even greater. Planners talked about potential US casualties of perhaps 250,000.

There was one alternative. The atom bomb.

Chapter 19

Final Defeat of Germany 1945

The winter of 1944/45 was particularly cold and wet. Famine stalked Holland and Belgium. Canadian and British troops suffered badly and trench foot was again rampant. Morale was low and there was an increase in desertions. Everyone knew that brave soldiers prepared to use their initiative or imbued with the fire of battle were the first to die. In both the British and American armies, persuading men to risk their lives in attack became increasingly difficult.

The military historian Professor Michael Howard, who was also a veteran of combat with the Wehrmacht, has written of the superior fighting ability of the German soldier over the British and American. The latter saw themselves as amateurs, drawn from a peaceful society, fighting the best professionals in the business. The German was also better armed and supported. The shell from an Allied Sherman tank would bounce off a German Tiger like a tennis ball. But a Sherman hit by a shell from a Tiger would not only be stopped but would probably catch fire. The German infantry anti-tank weapon was the extremely effective Panzerfaust. The Allied infantryman had only the very inferior Piat. The German soldier, like his Russian counterpart, was controlled by a ferocious discipline and draconian punishments. In the last months of the war, records show that 15,000 delinquent German soldiers were executed, with many more summary executions unrecorded.

German senior officers are also generally awarded higher marks than their Western opponents. But of course there are exceptions to all these generalities. Some British regiments did better than others. The American and British airborne troops were highly thought of. Brigadier Carver (later Field Marshal) was an outstanding leader of his brigade at the age of twenty-seven. The dynamic US General Patton was in the top rank and feared by the Wehrmacht. Some rate the brilliant US Airborne Major General James Gavin as one of the best. And then, of course, there was the great General Slim, and Field Marshal Lord Alanbrooke, perhaps the greatest of all.

One historian summed it up by writing that the Russian and German soldiers showed themselves better warriors but worse human beings. Whilst it is right to be realistic in appraising the fighting performance of British and American soldiers near the end of the war, it is also right to admire deeply the courage and endurance that so many so often displayed. Many are the stories of their sufferings. One must hope that succeeding generations will always remember and be deeply grateful for their heroic sacrifices, and perhaps most of all, for those who had to endure the pain and frustration of their physical and mental wounds for the rest of their lives.

As we have seen, the Soviet armies' conflict with the Wehrmacht dwarfed the campaign in the west in scale, intensity and savagery.

Between D-Day and the end of the war, the Western Allies lost 700,000 men killed, wounded or captured. In the same period the Soviet Union lost well over 2 million. Moreover, the ferocity of Soviet forces and their acceptance of huge casualties in destroying the German armies saved their allies from paying a much higher price. However, it is equally true that the tying down of large German forces in France and Italy, and also in Norway, greatly benefitted the Soviet Union.

In 1945, Air Marshal Harris's bombing campaign continued to use up large industrial resources while inflicting heavy damage if not devastation on German cities. It was conducted by hundreds of Lancaster aircraft every night. The campaign no longer had any strategic significance as Germany was slowly and surely losing the war. The Chief of the Air Staff Air Marshal Portal tried to change the policy and concentrate efforts on oil supply targets and so accelerate Germany's demise. This was the policy that the US Air Force tried to follow, not always successfully, in their daylight bombing. But Harris took scant notice of Air Staff directions and Portal was not strong enough to enforce them. Towards the end of the war, Churchill and others were beginning to feel uneasy about the slaughter of German civilians and the destruction of their cities to no military advantage. Little action was taken, but of course it is easier now to make moral judgements far away from the wartime heat of battle and the hatred of a cruel enemy. And so the terrible loss of gallant young life in Bomber Command continued.

The Russians started the final year of the war with a giant offensive along the whole 800 mile front line from the Baltic states down to Hungary and the Carpathian Mountains. Some 6.7 million men were deployed together with 14,000 tanks and 15,000 aircraft. Hitler could only counter with 4,800 tanks and 1,500 aircraft. He was particularly keen to defend Germany's fuel supplies in the Balkans and this took up seven of the eighteen Panzer divisions still available to him on the Russian front.

While the huge German Tiger tanks and the lighter faster Panthers were formidable, they had their electrical and hydraulic problems. They also used highly flammable petrol as their fuel. The Russian T-34 tank, initially inferior, had many improvements made as the war went on. Powered by diesel, after Kursk it was rearmed with an 85 mm gun and was fully able to take on the German armour.

On the southern front, the Hungarian Army stubbornly fought the Soviet invasion. Admiral Horthy, Regent of Hungary, managed to halt Eichmann's deportation of Jews, but not before 437,000 had been murdered, mostly at Auschwitz. In October, after secret talks with the Russians, he announced an armistice, which was never implemented as he was quickly removed from power. Many more Jews were then rounded up as slave labour and forced to march to Germany. Thousands died of exhaustion and brutal treatment on the way. About 60,000 were left behind in Budapest in a tiny ghetto.

One of the greatest operations to save the Jews was mounted by the Swedish diplomat Raoul Wallenberg. He issued tens of thousands of documents affording the bearer the protection of the Swedish government. He was later arrested by the Russians on trumped-up spying charges, and believed executed after the war. In this context, perhaps one should also mention Sir Nicholas Winton, the British diplomat who organised the rescue from the Nazis of 669 mostly Jewish children in Czechoslovakia, on the eve of war. There was also the more famous German industrialist Oskar Schindler. He saved 1,200 Jews from the Holocaust by employing them in his factories and bribing German officials.

Hitler ordered that Budapest be defended to the last. While the furious battle for the city went on until February 1945, the civilians inside slowly starved. The fearsome Hungarian right-wing militia had taken over the government, and one of their leaders was the notorious Fr András Kun. He used to give the command 'in the name of Christ, Fire!' In one of his most ghastly exploits he took a band of the militia to two Jewish hospitals and slaughtered all the patients and medical staff. A memorial to the thousands of Jews murdered in Budapest can be seen today on the banks of the Danube – a long row of empty concrete shoes where the victims had to remove their footwear before being shot.

Russian casualties were countless. A Hungarian officer described the Red Army soldiers impaled on a barbed wire barrier. One was still just alive. Both legs and lower arms were missing, the stumps encased in a mixture of soil and blood. His mouth managed to whisper 'Budapest' before the officer mercifully shot him. These were the soldiers who shot any wounded Germans they encountered and conducted an orgy of rape against Hungarian women.

On the Baltic coast, Hitler's refusal to allow a withdrawal resulted in the newly constituted Army Group Centre becoming partly trapped as well as part of Army Group North being bottled up in Latvia. However, under heavy air attack, the German Navy at great cost pulled off a feat of evacuation far larger than that of Dunkirk. Some 1.5 million civilians and four army divisions were embarked at Baltic ports and brought back to Germany. But when the German liner *Wilhelm Gustloff* was sunk by a Russian submarine, about 9,000 people, half of them children, perished – a huge number, typical of all the statistics of the long German/Soviet Union struggle. It is believed to have been the greatest loss of life on one ship ever known.

As the Russian colossus moved forward, the Germans conducted a disciplined fighting retreat of 300 miles. Warsaw was soon taken. Breslau and other cities were besieged and bypassed. The overall offensive came to an end in February with most of the Red Army temporarily exhausted at the end of long supply lines. The Sixth Panzer Army halted the Soviet advance from Hungary towards Vienna. But now the Soviet forces were only 44 miles from the suburbs of Berlin. The Stavka decided to defer the final assault until their armies were fully rested, resupplied and ready to go again into battle. The German High Command summoned thousands of men from every corner of the Reich for a last-ditch stand. Hundreds of 88 mm anti-aircraft batteries were also moved to reinforce Berlin's anti-tank defences.

However, Soviet forces in the north were still smashing into East Prussia and the northern half of Poland to protect Zhukov's flank. Their advance was characterised as usual by savage cruelty, rape and looting. There was now a tide of perhaps 8 million civilians fleeing westwards from East Germany's borders, terrified of the Red Army. After a long and violent battle the city of Konisberg fell to the Russians, who suffered heavy casualties. Facing a cruel imprisonment or death, hundreds, if not thousands of the surviving inhabitants committed suicide.

In February 1945, two months before his death, Roosevelt joined Churchill and Stalin for talks at Yalta in Crimea. The aim was to agree on plans for the post-war world. Roosevelt once again tried to bypass Churchill and persuade Stalin to adopt reasonable positions; the President made many derogatory remarks about the British and their leader in his charm offensive. Although he had little or no success he seemed to believe in the Soviet leader's good intentions. In 1944 at Moscow, Churchill had already tried to get favourable agreements with Stalin and had at least persuaded him that Greece should remain a Western interest. But with Eastern Europe under Soviet control, there was little that could be done to establish any political freedom in that area. Britain had gone to war to try to help Poland. Now, despite all Churchill's efforts, that country would remain under the iron control of another clever, evil dictator for many years. Roosevelt, that great friend of the West, was hopefully unaware before he died that his optimism for the future was largely misplaced. There was surprise and some regret that Churchill did not cross the Atlantic one more time to attend his funeral. The reasons for this decision are not known.

Adolf Hitler, looking increasingly old and unwell, continued to issue orders that in military terms were more and more unrealistic. He eventually accepted that defeat was inevitable and attributed it to the weakness of the German people. One of his last and craziest decisions followed. He gave orders for the utter physical destruction of all the facilities and infrastructure of his country as his forces were driven back. If this had been carried out it is difficult to see how the people of Germany could have survived the following winter. Luckily his all-powerful armaments minister Albert Speer, together with many generals, disregarded the orders. Mentioning Speer, one should add that he had been a major force in enabling Nazi Germany to continue the war for so long. Despite the years of huge aerial bombardment, German arms production was still increasing at the end of 1944. Along with the Wehrmacht, it was one of the few areas in the complex German war administration that was well organised and efficient, albeit much dependent on the extensive use of slave labour. The rest were generally riddled with conflicting priorities, muddled lines of authority often in competition, and sudden contradictory dictats from the Führer.

Although the outcome of the war had been in little doubt since the destruction of Army Group Centre in the summer of 1944, it was remarkable that the Wehrmacht, despite heavy casualties, continued to operate as an efficient, disciplined and effective fighting force. Four hundred thousand were killed in the first four months of 1945. But still they battled on to the end. Their steadfast performance was a tribute to their training and their traditions. It was no doubt reinforced by the many death sentences handed out on the Eastern Front for cowardice or desertion in the last year of the war. It is said that 10,000 unfortunate civilians and soldiers were hung from lamp posts by the military police in the battle for Berlin. The Red Army had also long been shooting anyone captured in SS uniform, as well as others. Spared prisoners fared little better. The 200,000 men of Germany's Army Group North cut off in Latvia kept fighting until May, when they were marched off to ten years' captivity, helping to rebuild a country they had devastated.

On the Western Front in 1945, Eisenhower's armies forced their way eastwards slowly and steadily but without enthusiasm in generally bad winter conditions. The fighting was heavy but there were also some quite large German surrenders. However, there were none in the Reichswald Forest, where the British fought a month-long difficult battle against fierce opposition, often in continuous wet, icy sleet. It was the nastiest battle since Normandy and became as miserable an experience as it was for the Americans in the Hürtgen.

Montgomery on reaching the Rhine began a slow and massive build-up, planning to be the first to cross. However, a US armoured division found one bridge at Remagen had not been demolished and rushed across. Hitler was furious, sacked Field Marshal Rundstedt once again, and ordered those responsible to be shot. Churchill,

Brooke and Montgomery watched the latter's forces crossing the next day. Brooke believed that the Prime Minister would have been happy to die in action there. It was certainly difficult to keep him back from the firing line.

Montgomery decided that alongside his crossing, there should be a large airborne operation to capture some high ground beyond the Rhine, together with bridges over the Ijssel River. Eisenhower agreed and US and British formations carried out Operation Varsity with thousands of gliders and paratroopers. It became a tragic disaster. As the air armada reached the dropping area it was met by some 350 anti-aircraft batteries with devastating results. Not only was it a failure that achieved little, it was a folly for which more than a thousand men paid with their lives. Gliders, which had been so successful on D-Day, were never again employed in the war.

In the winter of 1944/45, the dykes of Holland were opened for defensive purposes and much arable land flooded. Food supplies were commandeered by the Wehrmacht or refused import. Thousands of the able bodied had been deported for slave labour. Now the rest of the population were slowly starving. They longed for rescue by the British and Canadian armies, so near (their artillery could be heard), but moving slowly past. Eisenhower, supported by London and Washington, ruled that his operations must be governed by military not humanitarian considerations. That decision, together with bombing operations, cost many thousands of Dutch lives. Eventually, Allied air forces carried out air drops of food to prevent complete genocide.

Soon after this, 325,000 men of German Army Group B were surrounded in the Ruhr by General Bradley's forces and forced to surrender. Field Marshal Model escaped into a forest. He had heard that he was to be indicted for war crimes involving half a million people in Latvian war camps and he later shot himself. Bradley has been criticised by some for concentrating on the Ruhr, which no longer had much strategic significance, instead of forcing on into the heart of Germany.

It seemed now to be the start of a race to Berlin. Stalin's reaction was to send for Zhukov to work out an urgent overnight plan to hasten the Soviet assault on Germany's capital. He was utterly determined that the Soviet flag should fly over it. Aware through his spies of US atom bomb development, he also mistakenly believed there was a store of uranium in Berlin, which he wanted to deny the Americans.

But the race never happened. Eisenhower refused to consider the political importance of Berlin. He ordered 21st Army Group to head for Hamburg and Denmark. The main thrust of the American armies was to be to the south of Berlin. Churchill and his Chiefs of Staff, as well as Montgomery, were furious at what they saw as a change of plan. But Eisenhower had Roosevelt and General Marshall's support for what he considered a sensible military strategy. They also joined him in a wish not to upset Stalin, and the Soviet leader was informed of the plan. This made it more or less impossible to change it. The decision certainly avoided another bloody battle, which would have had little point since the post-war

Soviet occupation zone was already agreed to extend 100 miles west of Berlin.

Stalin replied to Eisenhower that for him Berlin was a secondary consideration. His main effort would be to link up with the US armies in the south. In fact the Stavka were working furiously on the detailed plans for an assault towards Berlin with 2.5 million men, over 6,000 tanks, and 7,500 aircraft. Presumably he did not care that his monstrous lie was bound to be found out soon.

As the Allied armies advanced from west and east they came across the full horrors of the Nazi regime in concentration camps and slave labour factories. They also caught up with those prisoners that the SS had not massacred but were being marched hundreds of miles, in severe winter weather, to avoid their liberation. Ill dressed, with little food, thousands died or were shot when unable to keep up. The Americans liberating Dachau were enraged by the horror confronting them and shot twenty-one of the guards. At Belsen, the British senior officer sent a strong detachment into the neighbouring town to bring the whole population back, at bayonet point, to bury 23,000 bodies on site, and 29,000 emaciated prisoners were evacuated. It is estimated that the futile movement of hundreds of thousands of prisoners from one concentration camp to another cost something like a quarter of a million lives.

Including prisoners of war, between 8 and 10 million souls were held in German captivity. American and British prisoners of war were mostly treated reasonably in accordance with the Geneva

Convention, which was supposed to govern the conduct of war. There was at least one exception when Hitler gave the infamous order to execute fifty of the prisoners who escaped from Stalag Luft III in 1944 in the famous 'Great Escape'. All the prisoners of war nevertheless suffered, sometimes for years, from suffocating boredom, hunger and cold. Officers were not liable for work but other ranks had to labour. The French, Polish and Italian POWs were treated more severely, but all knew they were fortunate compared with the Russians, who suffered great brutality. 5.7 million Red Army soldiers were captured during the war and 3.3 million died, including over half a million summarily shot soon after capture. Many of the rest held in slave labour camps were starved, frozen, shot or beaten to death.

While all this was going on, the US Fifth Army and British Eighth Army were advancing through the north of Italy. They were tying down large enemy forces. The Eighth Army had become an international organisation with divisions from Canada, India, Poland, South Africa and New Zealand. On 21 April, the Fifth Army captured Bologna while the Eighth Army took Ferrara and reached the Po River.

The Allied armies in the west continued their cautious approach across Germany, often without resistance, but with spasms of small but violent action in which men were killed just days before the war ended. Montgomery's armoured divisions, encouraged by Churchill, made more rapid advances in the north to ensure that Soviet forces could not threaten Denmark. On 11 April, US

General Simpson's Ninth Army reached the Elbe, poised to attack Berlin only 60 miles away. But he was ordered to halt and wait to shake hands with the approaching Red Army ten days later.

The Soviet advance into Germany was characterised by appalling scenes of rape, looting, murder and mindless destruction. Thousands of fleeing civilians were scattered or crushed by Soviet tanks, which paused only for many rapes to be carried out. From now until the end, the Soviet vengeance against Germans was one of great savagery. It was particularly so in Berlin, but however awful, not entirely surprising. For two years they had fought their way back through their own devastated country, with many towns and villages raised to the ground and their inhabitants starved or murdered. At least 2 million German women are thought to have been raped while their homes were destroyed and many subsequently died. But Germany's bloody deeds in the east had been little better than the Red Army's appalling behaviour.

On 16 April, the Soviet armies north and south of Berlin, led respectively by Marshal Zhukov and General Konev, commenced their final assault. Encouraged by Stalin, they were in fierce competition to win the city first. Some say Konev was the cleverer tactician, but Zhukov won. His crude and relentless assault started with an enormous bombardment by 22,000 guns and continued for three weeks, completely disregarding heavy casualties. With two German armies in the city the fighting was furious, and much of Berlin not already bombed was soon reduced to rubble. Many hundreds of Soviet tanks were destroyed by close range anti-tank weapons. About

100,000 civilians died, including about 5,000 suicides. It was all a terrible and unnecessary bloodletting since Germany had already lost the war and the battle could only have one result.

The German commander Field Marshal Schörner had many of his men shot for cowardice and declaimed to his officers how they needed to live up to their Führer's great trust. A few days later he deserted his army group, and wearing plain clothes, fled in a light aircraft to surrender to the Americans. He was handed over to the Russians and kept in prison for nine years.

On 28 April, Adolf Hitler married his partner Eva Braun in his underground bunker and two days later, shot himself while she took poison. Soon after this, his closest and most trusted minister Joseph Goebbels followed him. He and his wife Magda poisoned their six children and then took cyanide themselves. Hundreds of senior Nazi officials, ministers and generals followed suit and committed suicide.

On 2 May, Berlin surrendered. Six days later, Admiral Darlan, Hitler's appointed successor, surrendered all the forces of the Reich. The war in Europe was finally over.

Discussion of the reasons why Nazi Germany was defeated go beyond the scope of this short book. Suffice perhaps to say that while the Allies made strategic mistakes, Hitler made much greater ones. They were seized upon by the overwhelming might of the United States and the Soviet Union, helped by Britain magnificently led by the great Winston Churchill, and by the nations of its empire.

Chapter 20

The Atom Bomb

In the 1930s or earlier, scientists knew that elements contained vast amounts of energy in accordance with Einstein's equation: Energy = Mass x C^2 where C is the speed of light. A number developed the idea of a nuclear fission chain reaction. Bombarding the nucleus of a fissile atom with neutrons can split the atom into two new ones, releasing much energy plus two or three neutrons, which can perpetuate the process. At the beginning of the war, physicists on both sides and in America were well aware of the possibility of using nuclear fission as a weapon but not yet of how to do it.

The United Kingdom and America both set up research projects to ensure their development would outpace any parallel work in Germany. UK work went further ahead than that in the US, but to continue it large industrial resources were needed. And so, in 1943, it was agreed to join with the United States in the 'Manhattan project'. This became one of the largest industrial enterprises ever known, with many top scientists from Europe included in the team. Major investment was needed to separate the fissile Uranium-235 from the non-fissile isotope Uranium-238. (Isotope means the same element but with a different number of neutrons.) Tens of thousands of workers were employed on this task, most of whom had no idea of the significance of their work.

In July 1945, the first nuclear test of a plutonium bomb took place. The principle employed was to use explosives to force two non-critical masses together into a critical mass, which would set off the necessary chain reaction. The test released energy equivalent to 19,000 tons of TNT.

An ultimatum was then issued to Japan to either surrender or suffer complete and utter destruction. When Japan failed to comply, some advisers recommended dropping the bomb on unpopulated areas to demonstrate its power. But President Truman decided that a stronger message was needed. This is not the place to discuss the rights or wrongs of this decision, which has been argued about ever since. But perhaps we should remember that Allied leaders were still fighting a savage war that had killed over 50 million people. They were not sitting in the comfort of peacetime hindsight.

On 6 August 1945, a uranium atom bomb was detonated above Hiroshima and three days later a plutonium atom bomb was detonated above Nagasaki. These raids killed at least 135,000 Japanese outright, with a greater number dying later from related sickness. The cities were completely destroyed.

On 15 August, Emperor Hirohito announced Japan's surrender and the war was over.

The war undoubtedly caused and accelerated far-reaching changes in world civilisation. These included many political, geographical, social, scientific, technological and industrial advances. But it would take another whole book to examine these. Here let us just say that the Second World War was probably the most terrible event in the history of the world. It left the United Kingdom damaged, financially broken and heavily in debt. Germany lost a generation of her manhood, with the country itself physically and morally devastated. Japan's large army, navy and air force were in ruins, her major cities destroyed, and the country shamed before the world for generations to come. Altogether, the war cost the lives of between 50 and 60 million people, about half of them Russian. Let us pray that a world war will never happen again. With ever more powerful nuclear weapons, it is not impossible that it could end civilisation.

Appendix 1

Meetings of Great Power Leaders

1941 9–12 August Argentina Newfoundland (Riviera)	Churchill Roosevelt	Good personal rapport established. Atlantic Charter announced. US agrees to provide convoy escorts west of Iceland.
1942 22 December 1941– 14 January 1942 Washington (Arcadia)	Churchill Roosevelt	Close collaboration confirmed despite suspicions on both sides. Overriding priority for European War agreed.
22–25 June Washington	Churchill Roosevelt	Agreed cross-Channel invasion (Overlord) postponed. Private agreement of Churchill/Roosevelt to invade N. Africa (Operation Torch). Following Tobruk loss, generous US agreement to provide further new tanks and guns for Eighth Army.

12–17 August Moscow	Churchill Stalin	Their first meeting. Stalin initially bellicose then charming to Churchill. Agreement on exchange of information and technology.
1943 14–24 January Casablanca (Symbol)	Churchill Roosevelt	Strong difference of opinion between UK/US staffs. Eventually agree Overlord in 1944. Agree Sicily invasion. Plan joint bomber offensive. Agree Unconditional Surrender required.
14–15 May Washington (Trident)	Churchill Roosevelt	Further discussion on strategies and priorities.
12–24 August Quebec (Quadrant)	Churchill Roosevelt	SE Asia Command established. Invasion of Italy agreed. Secret nuclear research agreement. Overlord agreed for May 1944.

23–26 November Cairo (Sextant)	Churchill Roosevelt Chiang Kai-shek	First summit with Chinese Leader. Post-war arrangements in Far East. Somewhat ineffective discussion preparing for Teheran.
28 November–1 December Tehran (Eureka)	Stalin Churchill Roosevelt	First meeting of Big Three. Wide divergence between Churchill and Roosevelt and between UK/US staffs. Roosevelt sidelines Churchill in unsuccessful attempt to charm Stalin. Final strategy for European War discussion dominated by Stalin.
4–6 December Cairo	Churchill Roosevelt	Discussions with Turkish Prime Minister. Planning strategy in Far East. Churchill falls seriously ill.
1944 12–16 September Quebec (Octagon)	Churchill Roosevelt	Post-war plans discussed.

9–18 October Moscow (Tolstoy)	Stalin Churchill	Agreement on Churchill proposals for spheres of influence in post-war Europe. Churchill's attempts to obtain some post-war Polish independence meet stonewall.
1945 30 January– 2 February Malta	Churchill Roosevelt	Plan of final campaign of Europe agreed. Preparation for Yalta.
4–11 February Yalta, USSR (Argonaut)	Stalin Churchill Roosevelt	Roosevelt, old and frail, again sides with Stalin. No support for Churchill's repeated attempts to save Poland from total USSR subjugation. Agreement on United Nations organisation.
17 July–2 August Potsdam (Terminal)	Stalin Attlee Truman	Policy for post-war Germany agreed. Demand for Unconditional Surrender by Japan agreed.

Second World War Timeline

1936

March   Germany occupied Rhineland.

1938

March   Germany annexes Austria.

1939

15 March   Germany occupies Czechoslovakia.

24 August   Germany/Soviet Union Treaty.

1 September   Germany invades Poland.

3 September   UK declares war on Germany.

17 September   Aircraft carrier HMS *Courageous* sunk by U-boat.

14 October   Battleship HMS *Royal Oak* sunk by U-boat.

30 November   Russia invades Finland.

13 December   Battle of the River Plate.

1940

17 February   Prisoners released from Merchant Ship *Altmark*.

13 March   Soviet Union/Finland Peace Treaty.

9 April   Germany invades Norway and Denmark.

10 May   Winston Churchill becomes Prime Minister.

10 May   Germany invades France and Low Countries.

3 June	Dunkirk evacuation completed.
10 June	Italy declares war on UK.
18 June	France surrenders.
June	53 merchant ships sunk in Atlantic.
3 July	French fleet eliminated at Mers-el-Kébir.
23 August	Start of Battle of Britain.
September	US provides UK with 50 WWI destroyers.
2 October	Hitler postpones invasion of England indefinitely.
26 October	Italy invades Greece.
October	Admiral Dönitz starts wolfpack tactics in Atlantic.
30 October	Battle of Britain ends in British victory.
1 November	Start of Blitz – German bombing campaign against British cities.
11 November	Fleet Air Arm sink Italian ships in harbour at Taranto.
9 December	General Wavell's British and Commonwealth Eighth Army takes the offensive in N. Africa.
23 November	Italian forces driven out of Greece.

1941

8 February	Italian armies defeated by Eighth Army and Cyrenaica occupied.
12 February	General Rommel and first German Army units arrive in N. Africa.
28 March	Royal Navy victory in Mediterranean Battle of Matapan.
March	Cryptographers at Bletchley Park start breaking German Naval cyphers and provide vital intelligence for Battle of Atlantic.
6 April	Germany invades Greece and Yugoslavia.

13 April	Soviet Union and Japan sign Neutrality Pact.
25 April	British and Commonwealth detachment in Greece defeated.
10 May	Rudolf Hess flies from Germany to Scotland.
23 May	German battleship *Bismarck* sinks HMS *Hood*.
27 May	Royal Navy sinks *Bismarck*.
28 May	German paratroops capture Crete.
22 June	Germany invades Soviet Union (Operation Barbarossa).
June	General Rommel advances in N. Africa and defeats Wavell's forces.
June	Start of reduction in Atlantic shipping losses during second half of 1941.
July	US forces replace UK forces in Iceland.
July	US Navy starts escorting convoys in Western Atlantic.
14 November	Aircraft carrier HMS *Ark Royal* sunk by U-boat in Mediterranean.
25 November	Battleship HMS *Barham* sunk by U-boat in Mediterranean.
5 December	German Army forced to halt before Moscow.
8 December	Pearl Harbour: Japan attacks US fleet.
10 December	Battleship HMS *Prince of Wales* and battle cruiser HMS *Repulse* sunk by Japanese aircraft.
11 December	Hitler declares war on US.
18 December	Italian human torpedo group seriously damage battleships HMS *Queen Elizabeth* and HMS *Valiant* in Alexandria.
25 December	Hong Kong occupied by Japanese.

1942

18 Jan	Japan invades Burma.
January	Rommel defeated and Eighth Army retakes Cyrenaica.
20 January	Wannsee conference plans Holocaust.
15 February	Singapore surrenders.
February	German changes to naval ciphers prevent decryption. Merchant ship losses climb towards 100 per month.
19 February	Japanese air raid on Australia's Port Darwin.
February	Rommel retakes Cyrenaica.
6 May	Japanese complete occupation of Philippines.
May	Soviet forces in summer offensive suffer heavy defeats at Kharkov and in Crimea.
May	Japanese complete occupation of Burma.
4 June	US defeat of Japan at naval Battle of Midway.
21 June	Tobruk surrenders to Rommel.
30 June	Rommel halted at El Alamein in Egypt.
June	124 merchant ships sunk in the Atlantic.
4 July	Arctic convoy PQ17 disastrously ordered to scatter.
9 July	Germans take Sevastopol in South Russia.
19 August	Raid on Dieppe.
August	Australian troops in New Guinea halt Japanese advance on Port Moresby.
13 September	Battle of Stalingrad starts.
4 November	General Montgomery's victory at Battle of El Alamein.
8 November	Operation Torch. Allied landings in Morocco and Algeria.
December	Capture of U-boat documents allows renewed decryption of German naval signal traffic.

1943

January	Guadalcanal and Papua Guinea recaptured by US forces.
February	Increasing number of long-range Liberator aircraft from US allows closure of 'air gap' in central Atlantic.
2 February	German Sixth Army surrenders in Stalingrad.
20 March	21 ships in two adjacent Atlantic convoys sunk in one night.
March	Total of 82 merchant ships lost in Atlantic and 15 U-boats destroyed.
12 May	German surrender in Tunisia ends operations in N. Africa.
24 May	Catastrophic U-boat losses of 41 boats in one month forces Admiral Dönitz to withdraw from the Atlantic. Allies win the Battle of the Atlantic.
27 May	First of succession of bombing raids that destroy Hamburg.
10 July	Allies invade Sicily.
23 July	German defeat in major tank battle at Kursk.
26 July	Mussolini deposed.
23 August	Russians retake Kharkov.
3 September	Allied invasion of Italy.
8 September	Italy surrenders.
9 September	Allied landing at Salerno.
8 November	Soviet forces retake Kiev.

1944

22 January	Allied landing at Anzio.
15 February	Allied bombing destroys Monte Cassino monastery.

19 March	German troops occupy Budapest.
April	Japan launches Ichi-Go offensive in China.
9 May	Soviet Army retakes Sevastopol and Crimea.
14 May	Allied forces break through Gustav Line in Italy.
23 May	Japanese finally defeated at Kohima.
4 June	Allies enter Rome.
6 June	D-Day.
22 June	Soviet Union launches major offensive (Operation Bagration).
13 June	V-1 cruise missile attacks on London start.
3 July	Soviet forces capture Minsk, 200 miles from start of Bagration. German Army Group Centre effectively destroyed.
20 July	Plot to assassinate Hitler fails.
October	Japanese China offensive ends in major defeat of Chiang Kai-shek's nationalist forces and capture of US air bases.
1 August	Warsaw uprising of Polish Jews.
15 August	Allied forces land in south of France.
20 August	German Seventh Army and Fifth Panzer Army defeated in Normandy.
25 August	De Gaulle Free French forces liberate Paris.
2 September	Soviet forces secure Bucharest and Ploesti oil fields.
3rd September	British troops enter Brussels.
8 September	V-2 rocket attacks on London start.
15 September	General MacArthur's army launches assault on Philippines.
27 September	British paratroops at Arnhem forced to surrender.
2 October	Warsaw uprising ends in total defeat of Polish Jews.

12 October	German forces withdraw from Greece.
23–26 October	Major Japanese naval losses at Battle of Leyte Gulf.
25 October	Japanese start 'kamikaze' air attacks.
16 December	Start of Ardennes offensive (Battle of the Bulge).

1945

3 January	Battle of the Bulge ends in German defeat.
12 January	Start of major Soviet offensive across whole North to South front.
12 February	Budapest falls to Soviet troops.
13 February	Bomber Command destroys Dresden.
7 March	Allies cross Rhine.
10 March	Major US air raid on Tokyo.
20 March	General Slim's British and Indian Fourteenth Army takes Mandalay.
26 March	US forces complete capture of Iwo Jima.
2 April	Japanese battleship *Yamato* sunk by US aircraft.
5 April	US forces encircle German Army Group B in the Ruhr.
10 April	Soviet troops reach Vienna.
12 April	President Roosevelt dies. Harry S. Truman becomes President.
20 April	Battle of Berlin starts.
25 April	Berlin surrounded by Soviet forces, US and Soviet troops meet on the Elbe.
30 April	Hitler commits suicide.
2 May	Berlin surrenders.
3 May	Fourteenth Army takes Rangoon. Japanese forces expelled from Burma.

8 May	Final surrender of Germany. End of war in Europe.
22 June	Okinawa's resistance ends.
6 August	Atom bomb dropped on Hiroshima.
9 August	Atom bomb dropped on Nagasaki.
14 August	Japan surrenders. End of Second World War.

Index

Aachen, 140
Abbeville, 13
Achilles, HMNZ, 10
Admiral Hipper, 11
Admiralty, the, 42, 45, 58, 155
Afrika Corps, 32, 35, 36, 96, 97, 98
'Air gap', 39, 189
Air raid, 23, 25, 67, 84–5, 86, 90, 155, 178,
     188, 189, 191
     see also Blitz
     blackout, 25
     shelter, 25, 133
     wardens, 25
Aircraft factories, 22, 27
Ajax, HMS, 10
Alamein *see* Battle of
Alanbrooke, FM Lord, 162
     see also Brooke, Gen Sir Alan
Alexander, Gen Harold, 101, 107, 111,
     112, 144
Algeria, 19, 99, 188
Allies, 30, 63, 64, 67, 84, 90, 98, 100–101,
     103, 107, 108, 116, 121, 122, 126, 129,
     135–6, 141, 163, 175, 178, 188, 189,
     190, 191
     aircraft/airfields, 108, 120, 121, 143, 172
     forces, 31, 65, 68, 86, 97, 99–100, 101, 105,
          107, 108–10, 111–12, 127, 129, 131,
          134–6, 140, 141, 147, 148, 158, 161, 163,
          170, 172–3, 188, 189, 190, 191
     headquarters, 142
Altmark, 10, 185
America *see* US/USA
Anti-aircraft/AA defences, 25, 36, 86, 87,
     154–5, 166, 170
Anti-personnel devices, 140
Anti-submarine ships/defences, 6, 8, 9,
     39–40, 83
Anti-tank gun/defences, 8, 36, 54, 109, 117,
          129, 161, 166, 174
Antwerp, 136, 137, 144
Anzio *see* Battle of
Arakan, 77–8, 145, 148
Arctic convoys *see* Convoys
Arctic Star, 59
Ardennes, 12, 140, 141, 191
Ark Royal, 35, 187
Arnhem, 137–9, 190
Atlantic *see* Battle of
Atlantic Charter, 30, 181
Atlantic convoys *see* Convoys
Atom bomb, 102, 159, 171, 177–9, 192
Auchinleck, Gen, 34, 36, 37
Auschwitz, 164
Australia/Australian, 5, 65, 66, 67, 74–5, 188
     forces, 17, 33, 35, 65, 74–5, 96, 97, 154, 188
Austria, 3, 185
Austro-Hungarian Empire, 1
Axis powers, 5, 13, 97, 100, 107

B29 Superfortress, 149, 150
Babi Yar, 52
Balkans, 100, 108, 109, 122, 164
Baltic coast/states, 123, 164, 166
Baltic Fleet, Soviet, 54–5
Baltic Sea, 10
Barham, HMS, 35, 187
Bari, 110–11
Barnet, Correlli, 42
Bastogne, 142–3
Bataan Peninsula, 66
Battle of:
     Alamein, 17, 96–8, 188
     Anzio, 111–12, 125, 189
     the Atlantic, 5, 9–10, 17, 22, 36, 39–46, 47,
          64, 85, 98, 103–106, 125, 186, 187, 188,
          189
     Berlin, 169, 171, 174–5

Britain, 4, 7, 18, 21–4, 84, 186
Bulge, the, 142–3, 191
Guadalcanal, 73–4, 189
Kursk, 116–18, 189
Leyte Gulf, 150–1, 191
Matapan, 32, 186
Meiktila, 153
Midway, 71–3, 188
Okinawa, 156–8, 192
River Plate, the, 9–10, 185
Stalingrad, 91–3, 188
Beaverbrook, Lord, 22
Belgium, 9, 12, 18, 126, 161
Belgrade, 122–3
Belorussia, 121
Belsen, 172
Berlin, 23, 79, 132, 166, 169, 171–2,
174–5, 191
see also Battle of
Bevin, Ernest, 27
Bismarck, battleship, 41–2, 187
Bismarck, Chancellor Otto von, 1
Black Sea, 89, 119
Bletchley Park, 41, 45, 46, 97, 116, 141, 186
Blitz, the, 25, 27, 186
Blitzkrieg, 12
Bologna, 173
Bolsheviks *see* Soviet Union
Bomber Command, 8, 42, 83–7, 163, 191
see also British Air Force
Borneo, 66–7, 158
Bouncing bomb, 85–6
Bradley, Gen Omar, 107, 128, 129, 134, 136,
141, 142, 144, 171
Braun, Eva, 175
Breslau, 166
Brest, 42
Britain, 1–4, 5–6, 7, 8, 9, 11, 12, 13, 14, 15,
16, 17–19, 21–4, 25–30, 31, 36, 42, 57, 64,
65, 78, 80, 83–5, 89, 98, 99, 100, 103, 104,
105, 115, 135, 167, 175
Home Front:
civil defence, 27
evacuation, 27
factories, 22, 27
food production/Dig for Victory, 26
Home Guard, 27, 78
rationing, 25–6, 106

Women's Land Army, 27
see also Battle of
British:
Air Force/Royal Air Force, 8, 16, 17, 21,
103, 127, 135, 155, 170
Bomber Command, 8, 42, 83–7, 163, 191
Desert Air Force, 96, 98, 101
Army, 7, 13, 15
6th Airborne Division, 128
7th Armoured Division (Desert Rats),
31
21st Army Group, 17–18, 128, 136, 142,
171
IV Corps, 151
XV Corps, 77–8, 145
XXX Corps, 138
XXXV Corps, 151
conscription, 7, 26, 27
Eighth Army, 17, 34, 35, 37, 96, 97–8,
101, 107, 108, 112, 173, 181, 186, 188
expeditionary force (BEF), 9, 14
First Army, 100
Fourteenth Army, 78, 145, 148, 151, 153,
191
Irish Guards, 111
Royal Artillery, 98
Royal Engineers (Sappers), 97
Royal Sussex Regiment, 110
Second Army, 18–19, 128, 129
Sherwood Foresters, 111
West Kent Regiment, 146, 147
Navy *see* Royal Navy
British Empire, 1, 5, 14, 17, 29, 67, 175
British Expeditionary Force (BEF) *see* British
Army
Brooke, Gen Sir Alan, 15, 29, 98, 100,
101–102, 108, 119, 125, 144, 154, 170
see also Alanbrooke, FM Lord
Brown, Tommy, 45–6
Browning, Lt Gen 'Boy', 139
Buckner, Lt Gen Simon Bolivar, 158
Budapest, 122–3, 164, 165, 190, 191
Bulgaria, 122–3
Bulge, the *see* Battle of
Burma, 17, 67, 70, 76–7, 78, 145, 146, 148–9,
151, 153, 188, 191
Army, 69, 77
Railway, 65–6, 68

Road, 61, 67, 151
Butcher of Prague *see* Heydrich

Caen, 129, 130, 134
Cairo, 37, 119, 183
Calais, 126, 130
Campbeltown, HMS, 43
Canada, 39
    armed forces, 5, 17, 41, 90, 128, 134, 135,
        137, 161, 170, 173
    Newfoundland, 30, 181
Cape Matapan, 32, 186
Carpathian Mountains, 164
Carver, Brig Michael, 162
Casablanca, 100, 103, 182
Caucasus, 49, 89
Chamberlain, Neville, 3–4, 11
Channel *see* English Channel
Chennault, Gen, 70
Cherbourg Peninsula, 128, 129–30, 137
Chiang Kai-shek, Gen, 61, 67, 149, 183, 190
Chiefs of Staff, 12, 28, 29, 42, 55, 61, 85, 90,
    144, 154, 171
China, 5, 61, 62, 64, 67, 149, 156, 190
Chindits, 77, 145, 148
Chindwin River, 151
Chuikov, Gen, 91, 92
Churchill, Winston, 4, 10, 11–12, 14, 15,
    16–17, 18, 19, 24, 25, 27, 28–9, 30, 34,
    36–7, 42, 44, 57, 63–4, 70, 83, 85, 90, 96,
    98–9, 100, 101–102, 103, 104, 107–108,
    109, 118–19, 122, 125, 127, 139, 145, 153,
    154, 163, 167–8, 169–70, 171, 173, 175,
    181, 182, 183, 184, 185
Clark, Gen Mark, 108–109, 111, 112
Clark Field, 64
Coastal Command *see* Royal Air Force
Commandos, 43, 90
Communism/communists, 2, 52, 61, 121,
    122, 140, 149
Concentration camps, 9, 80, 121–2, 172
Conscription, 3, 7, 26–7, 63, 68, 135
Convoys, 9, 35, 40–41, 43, 44–5, 54–5, 57–9,
    75, 83, 90, 95–6, 104–106, 116, 181, 187,
    188, 189
Coral Sea, 71
Corregidor Island, 66
Cossack, HMS, 10

Courageous, HMS, 9, 185
Coventry, 25
Crete, 33–4, 36, 187
Croydon, 133
Cunningham, ADM, 32, 33–4, 35
Cyrenaica *see* Libya
Czechoslovakia, 2, 3, 4, 80–1, 165, 185

Dachau, 172
Dambusters raid, 75, 85
Danube River, 122, 165
Darlan, ADM, 99, 175
Dauntless dive-bomber, 73
D-Day, 107, 112, 127, 128, 135, 140, 163,
    170, 190
De Gaulle, General, 15–16, 135, 190
Dempsey, Gen Miles, 128
Denmark, 10, 171, 173, 185
Desert Rats *see* British Army, 7th Armoured
    Division
Desert War, 33, 35, 36–7, 96–8, 101
Devastator torpedo bomber, 72
Dieppe Raid, 90, 125, 188
Dimapur, 146
Disease, 65–6, 68, 70, 80, 110, 140, 142, 145,
    148, 158, 161
Dnieper River, 118
Don River, 91
Dönitz, ADM, 40, 45, 105, 186, 189
Doodlebug *see* V-1 flying bomb
Doss, Cpl Desmond, 157
Dowding, ACM Sir Hugh, 22
Dresden, 86, 191
Dunkirk, 13, 14–15, 16, 18, 166, 186

East Africa, 31
Eastern Front, 116, 118, 169
Eastern Mediterranean, 32, 83, 108
Edward VII, King, 1
Egypt, 31, 34, 36, 96, 108, 188
    see also Cairo
    see also El Alamein
Eifel Forest, 141
Eighth Army *see* British Army
Eindhoven, 138–9
Einsatzgruppen *see* German SS
Eire, 5
Eisenhower, Gen Ike, 99, 100, 101, 127, 128,

136, 137, 141, 142, 144, 169, 170, 171, 172
El Alamein, 17, 37, 96–8, 188
Elbe River, 173–4, 191
England, 15, 21, 24, 125, 186
English Channel, 21, 22–3, 100, 101, 107,
    119, 126, 127, 137, 141, 181
Enigma machines, 41, 45
    see also Ultra
Enlistment, 26–7
Enterprise, USS, 72
Estonia, 54, 123
Execution/extermination, 9, 52, 72, 77, 80–1,
    162
    camps *see* Concentration camps
Exeter, HMS, 10

Falaise Gap, 134
Far East, 36, 61–78, 100, 145–59, 183
Fasson, Lt, 45–6
Ferrara, 173
Fighter Command *see* Royal Air Force
Filipino soldiers, 66
Finland, 185
First World War, 1, 5, 6, 13, 125
Flying Fortress, 84
Force H *see* Royal Navy
Forrestal, James, 155
France, 1, 4, 5, 8, 9, 12, 13, 14–17, 18, 22, 32,
    42, 43, 47, 83, 90, 98–9, 101, 107, 112, 116,
    119, 125–31, 135–6, 137, 163, 185, 186, 190
    army, 5, 12–13, 15, 16, 99, 100
    Free French forces, 16, 99, 135, 140, 190
    navy, 18–19, 186
    resistance/Maquis, 19, 127, 130
    Vichy government, 16, 19, 99
Frankfurt, 136

Gas chambers, 80
Gavin, Maj Gen James, 162
Geneva Convention, 172–3
German:
    Air Force, 15, 23, 33, 57
        aircraft, 23, 31, 58
        see also Luftwaffe, Messerschmitt
    Army, 1, 2, 3, 5–6, 8, 12–13, 15, 37, 51, 54,
        91, 92, 109, 111, 116, 118, 122, 131, 134,
        166, 186, 187, 189, 190, 191
        Army Group B, 126, 171, 191

Army Group Centre, 49, 50, 54, 55, 120,
    166, 168, 190
Army Group North, 49, 54, 166, 169
Army Group South, 49, 89, 92, 119
Panzer Army, 12, 13, 14, 32, 49, 54, 55, 91,
    97, 100, 126, 129, 130, 134, 138, 141,
    142, 143, 164, 166, 190
paratroopers, 33, 187
OKH (Oberkommando des Heeres), 55
Seventh Army, 134, 190
Sixth Army, 91, 189
Tenth Army, 112
    see also Afrika Corps
Gestapo, 3, 28, 132
Navy (Kriegsmarine), 6, 10, 11, 22–3, 41,
    43, 44, 166
    submarines *see* U-boat
SS (SchutzStaffel), 3, 79, 81, 130, 172
    Einsatzgruppen, 51, 52, 79
surrender, 101
Waffen-SS, 3, 121
Wehrmacht/OKW (Oberkommando der
    Wehrmacht), 5, 48, 51, 52, 58–9, 89,
    109, 112, 118, 121, 122, 123, 161, 162,
    168, 170
Germany, 1–4, 5, 9, 10–11, 13, 14, 16, 21,
    27–8, 30, 33, 42, 47, 51, 57, 59, 62, 63, 84,
    85, 87, 89, 97, 109, 119, 121, 122, 132, 133,
    136, 141, 143, 161–75, 179, 184, 185, 186,
    187, 192
Gestapo *see* German
Gibraltar, 35, 95–6
Gibson, Wg Cdr Guy, 86
Glowworm, destroyer, 11
Goebbels, Joseph, 28, 30, 175
George VI, King, 126
Goering, Field Marshal, 5–6, 21–2, 92
'Gold' Beach, 128
Gort, Gen Lord, 95
Graf Spee, battleship, 9–10
Grave, 128
Great Britain *see* Britain
Greece, 31, 32, 33, 34, 36, 122, 139, 140, 167,
    186, 187, 191
Gretton, VADM Sir Peter, 40
Guadalcanal *see* Battle of
Guingand, Gen 'Freddie' de, 144
Gulag *see* Siberia

Gurkha, 69, 145, 148
Gustav line, 109–10, 111–12, 190

Hacksaw Ridge, 157
Haguro, cruiser, 158
Halifax, Lord, Foreign Secretary, 13–14
Hamburg, 86, 171, 189
Hamilton, Duke of, 30
Hara-kiri, 157–8
Harman, L Cpl John VC, 147
Harris, ACM 'Bomber', 42, 85, 127, 163
Harwood, Cdre, 10
Hawaii, 62
    see also Pearl Harbour
Hellcat fighter aircraft, 150
Heroes of Telemark, The, 19
Hess, Rudolf, 29–30, 187
Heydrich, Reinhard, 'Butcher of Prague', 51,
    79–80
Himmler, Heinrich, 51–2, 79, 81, 121
Hirohito, Emperor, 62, 178
Hiroshima, 178, 192
Hitler, Adolf, 1, 2–4, 5, 10, 12, 14, 16, 21, 23,
    24, 25, 29, 30, 32, 44, 47–9, 52, 54, 55, 63,
    79, 89, 90–1, 92, 93, 97, 100, 101, 116, 117,
    118, 119–20, 123, 126, 132, 133, 135, 141,
    164, 165, 166, 168, 169, 173, 175, 186, 187,
    190, 191
Hitler Youth, 3
Hodges, Gen Courtney, 142
Holland, 9, 126, 161, 170
Holocaust, 79–81, 165, 188
Home Guard *see* Britain, Home Front
Hong Kong, 64, 187
Hood, HMS, 41, 187
Hornet, USS, 72
Horrocks, Gen Brian, 138–9
Horthy, ADM Miklós, 164
Horton, ADM Sir Max, 44
Hungarian Army, 89, 164, 165
Hungary, 164, 166
    see also Austro-Hungarian Empire
Hurricane, fighter plane, 4, 8, 22, 23, 145
Hürtgen Forest, 140, 169

Iceland, 39, 181, 187
Ichi-Go offensive, 149, 190
Ijssel River, 170

Illustrious, HMS, 32
Imphal, 146, 148
India/Indian, 5, 34, 67, 69, 70, 146, 148
    armed forces, 17, 68, 78, 96, 145, 146,
        173, 191
Indian Ocean, 10, 154
Intelligence, 41, 49, 97, 103, 116, 129, 132,
    141, 186
    see also Ultra
Iran, 34, 57
Iraq, 34
Irrawaddy River, 152
Irwin, Gen Stafford LeRoy, 77, 78
Italy/Italian, 5, 17, 31, 32, 33, 83, 87, 95, 96,
    101, 102, 107–13, 117, 163, 173, 182, 186,
    187, 189, 190
    Army, 31, 89, 92
    Navy, 31–2, 35, 36
    see also Sicily
    see also Taranto
Iwo Jima, 155, 191

Japan/Japanese, 5, 48, 61–78, 101, 132, 145,
    146, 148, 149, 150, 151, 155, 156, 157–9,
    178, 184, 187, 188, 190, 191, 192
    Air Force, 145, 150, 151, 158, 179
    Army, 77, 145, 146–7, 148–9, 150, 152–3,
        158, 179
    High Command, 150
    Navy, 7, 150, 157, 179
    Neutrality Pact, 62, 187
Java, 67
Jews, 3, 9, 47, 52, 79–81, 131, 164–5, 190
Joint Chiefs of Staff, 28, 144
Joyce, William (Lord Haw Haw), 28
Jungle, 65, 67–8, 73, 74, 77, 145–6, 148
'Juno' Beach, 128

Kamikaze, 156, 157, 191
Kasserine Pass, 100
Katyusha rocket launcher, 117
Kennedy, Lt J.F., 76
Kent, 23, 133
Kenya, 31
Kesselring, FM, 109, 111
KGB *see* Soviet Union
Kharkov, 89, 115, 116, 118, 188, 189
Kiev, 49, 52, 54, 118, 189

Kimura, Gen Heitaro, 152
King, ADM Ernest, 63
Kluge, FM Günther von, 132
Kohima, 146, 148, 190
Kokoda Trail, New Guinea, 17, 74
Konev, Gen Ivan, 118, 174
Konisberg, 167
Kretschmer, Otto, 44
Kriegsmarine *see* German Navy
Kun, Fr András, 165
Kursk, 116, 118, 164, 189
    see also Battle of

Lancaster bomber, 85, 163
Latvia, 123, 166, 169, 171
Lebensraum, 2, 47, 52
Leese, Gen Oliver, 153, 154
Lend-Lease *see* United States
Leningrad, 49, 54, 55, 115, 119
Lexington, USS, 71
Leyte, island, 150, 151, 191
Leyte Gulf *see* Battle of
Liberator, 8, 43, 103, 104, 189
Liberty ships, 103
Libya, 31, 34, 35
Lightning, 76
Lithuania, 123
London, 23, 25, 65, 132, 133, 144, 170, 190
Longfellow, 28
Lord Haw Haw *see* Joyce, William
Lorient, 42
Low Countries, 12, 67, 185
Luftwaffe, 6, 11, 12, 23, 24, 54, 89, 92, 120, 143
    see also Stuka
Luzon, 151, 158

MacArthur, Gen Douglas, 66, 70–1, 74–5, 150, 151, 190
Macintyre, Capt Donald, 44
Maginot Line, 8, 12
Malaya, 64, 65
Malaya, battleship, 35
Malta, 35, 95–6, 108, 184
Mandalay, 151–3, 191
Manhattan project, 177
Manila, 151
Manstein, FM Erich von, 115, 117, 119

Mao Zedong, 61, 149
Maquis, 127, 130
Mariana Islands, 149–50
Marshall, Gen G.C., 28–9, 90, 98–9, 101, 107, 108, 119, 127, 158, 171
Mass graves, 115, 123
Matapan *see* Battle of
Medal of Honor, 157
Mediterranean, 31–7, 39, 45–6, 83, 95, 98, 99, 100, 107, 108, 144, 186, 187
Meiktila *see* Battle of
Mein Kampf, 1–2, 47
Merchant Navy, British, 10, 27, 33, 40, 105
Merchant ships, 10, 33, 35, 39, 41, 44, 45, 58, 64, 95–6, 104, 105, 185, 186, 188, 189
Mers-El-Kébir, 19, 186
Messerschmitt, 30
Messervy, Gen Frank, 152
Metz, 140
Meuse River, 141, 143
Midway *see* Battle of
Midway Island, 71–3, 188
Minsk, 49, 50, 190
Model, FM Walter, 171
Monte Cassino, 109–10, 189
Montevideo, 10
Montgomery, Gen Bernard, 37, 96–8, 99, 107, 108, 110, 127, 128, 129, 130, 134, 136, 137–9, 142, 144, 169–70, 171, 173, 188
Morgan, Lt Gen Sir Frederick, 125
Morocco, 99, 119, 188
Moscow, 49, 54, 55, 56, 63, 89, 90, 116, 139, 167, 182, 184, 187
Mountbatten, ADM Louis, 78, 101–102, 153–4
Mountbatten, Lt Philip, 158
Mulberry harbours, 126
Mussolini, Benito, 5, 31, 108, 189
Mustang fighter, 84
Mustard gas, 110–11
Myitkyina, 146

Nagasaki, 178, 192
Naples, 109
Narvik, Norway, 11
National Socialist Party *see* Nazi Party
Nazi Party/Nazis, 1, 3, 14, 19, 30, 62, 81, 123, 135, 165, 168, 172, 175

Nazi/Soviet pact, 49
Netherlands, The, 18, 137–8
New Guinea, 17, 70, 71, 75, 150, 188
New Zealand, 5, 10, 17, 33, 96, 97, 173
Newfoundland *see* Canada
Nijmegen, 138–9
Nimitz, ADM, 63, 70–1, 154
NKVD *see* Soviet Union
Non-aggression/Neutrality Pact, 2, 62, 187
Normandy, 120, 125–44, 169, 190
North Africa, 17, 99–102
North Atlantic, 39–46
Norway, 10–11, 12, 18, 19, 44, 57, 59, 83, 100,
   126, 163, 185
Norsk Hydro plant, 19
Nuclear fission/bomb, 17, 19, 177–9, 182,
   192

OKH (Oberkommando des Heeres) *see*
   Germany Army
OKW (Oberkommando der Wehrmacht) *see*
   German Wehrmacht
Ohio, SS, 96
Oil/fuel, 9, 34, 40, 44, 45, 47, 49, 62, 67, 85,
   89, 122, 163, 190
Okinawa, 156–8, 192
   see also Battle of
'Omaha' Beach, 128, 129
Operations:
   Bagration, 120, 190
   Barbarossa, 47–56, 120, 187
   Jedburgh, 130
   Market Garden, 137–9
   Overlord, 98, 101, 108, 119, 181, 182
   Pedestal, 95–6
   Sea Lion, 24
   Torch, 99–100, 107, 125, 181, 188
   Varsity, 170
Oradour, 130
Orne River, 128

Pacific, 71, 75, 76, 149, 155
Panzer Army *see* German Army
Panzerfaust, 161
Papua, 71, 74, 189
Patton, Gen, 99, 100, 107, 126, 128, 134, 136,
   137, 140, 143, 144, 162
Paulus, Gen, 91, 92

Pearl Harbour, 62, 64, 67, 71, 187
Pétain, Marshal, 16, 99
Philippines, 64, 66, 70–1, 75, 150, 151, 188,
   190
Phoney war (1940), 9, 10
PLUTO, 127
Plutonium bomb *see* Atom bomb
Po River, 173
Po Valley, 112
Poland/Polish, 2, 4, 8, 9, 12, 15, 18, 22, 52,
   79, 81, 115, 119, 121, 138, 139, 167, 173,
   184, 185, 190
Port Moresby, New Guinea, 17, 74, 188
Portal, AM Charles, 163
Pound, ADM, 58
Prince of Wales, HMS, 36, 64, 187
Propaganda, 27, 28, 81, 115
Prien, Günther, 9
Pripet Marshes, 49, 120
Prisoners/POWs, 10, 13, 16, 31, 33, 50, 51,
   53, 65–6, 76, 80, 89, 101, 117, 123, 143,
   151, 156, 169, 172–3, 185
Prussia, 167
Puller, Gen Lewis Burwell, 74

Quebec, 101, 182, 183
Queen Elizabeth, battleship, 35, 187
Quisling, Maj, 11

Rabaul, 150
Radar, 7, 22, 39, 103
Ramsay, VADM/ADM, 14, 127
Randle, Capt Jack VC, 147
Rangoon, 68, 151, 153, 191
Red Army *see* Soviet Union
Refugees, 13
Reich *see* Germany
Reichswald Forest, 169
Remagen, 169
Repulse, HMS, 36, 64, 187
Rhine River, 137–8, 139, 169, 170, 191
Rhineland, 3, 185
Rhodes, 108
River Plate, the *see* Battle of
Romania, 92, 122
Rome, 109, 111, 112, 190
Rommel, Gen Erwin, 32, 34, 35, 36, 37, 95,
   96, 97, 98, 100, 101, 126, 132, 186, 187, 188

Roope, Lt Cdr G.B., 11
Roosevelt, Franklin D., 16, 18, 28–9, 30, 37, 75, 89, 98–9, 101, 102, 103, 107, 118, 119, 127, 150, 158, 167, 171, 181, 182, 183, 184, 191
Rotterdam, 84
Royal Air Force *see* British Air Force
    Bomber Command, 8, 42, 83–7, 163, 191
    Coastal Command, 8, 39, 41, 85, 103
    Fighter Command, 22
    see also British Air Force
Royal Navy, The, 7, 9, 10, 31–2, 33, 35, 41–2, 57–9, 65, 95, 152, 154, 155, 186, 187
    see also Scapa Flow
Royal Oak, HMS, 9, 185
Ruhr, The, 85, 136, 137, 171, 191
Rundstedt, General Von, 14, 120, 126, 141, 169
Russia *see* Soviet Union

Sabotage *see* Special Operations Executive
Saint-Lô, 134
Saipan, 149, 150
Salerno Bay, 109, 125, 189
SAS *see* Special Air Service
Scapa Flow, 9
Scharnhorst, battleship, 59
Scheldt Estuary, 136
Schindler, Oskar, 165
Schörner, FM Ferdinand, 175
Scotland, 30, 187
Seabee construction battalions, 75
Sebastopol, 91
Sedan, 12–13
Senegalese, 13
Siberia, 48, 53–4
    Gulag, 53
Sicily, 33, 95, 101, 107, 108, 117, 182, 189
Simpson, Gen William Hood, 173–4
Singapore, 36, 64–5, 188
Sittang River, 69
Slaves/slave labour, 16, 47, 52, 67, 80, 121, 125, 133, 164, 168, 170, 172, 173
Slavs, 47, 52
Slim, Lt Gen William, 69, 76–8, 119, 145, 146, 152, 153–4, 162, 191
Smolensk, 49, 51, 115
Snelling, Maj Gen Alf, 152
Solomon Islands, 66–7, 73

    see also Guadalcanal
Somerville, ADM, 35
South Africa, 5, 17, 96, 173
South Atlantic, 10
South East Asia, 62, 65, 67, 71
    Command, 101
Soviet Union, 2, 8, 30, 47–56, 57, 59, 62, 89–93, 115–23, 139–40, 162, 163, 164, 166, 167, 171–2, 173, 174–5, 185, 187, 188, 189, 190, 191
    Baltic Fleet, 54
    Bolsheviks, 30, 47
    Great Patriotic War, 54, 92
    KGB, 50
    NKVD, 50, 51, 91, 122
    Red Army, 50–1, 55, 59, 116, 117, 121–3, 132, 165, 166, 167, 169, 173, 174
    Stavka, 50, 120, 123, 166, 172
Special Air Service (SAS), 36
Special Operations Executive (SOE), 19
Speer, Albert, 168
Spitfire fighter plane, 4, 8, 22, 23, 84, 95, 145
Spruance, ADM Raymond, 149–50
SS (SchutzStaffel) *see* German
St Nazaire, 43
Stalin, Joseph, 2, 9, 30, 48, 49, 50, 52, 53–4, 58, 89–90, 91, 99, 101, 115, 116, 118, 119, 120, 123, 139–40, 167, 171–2, 174, 182, 183, 184
Stalingrad, 91–3, 101, 115, 188, 189
    see also Battle of
Stavelot, 143
Stilwell, Gen 'Vinegar' Joe, 61, 68–9, 70
Strasbourg, 140
Stuka dive-bomber, 12, 121
Submarine, 6, 7, 8, 9, 35, 39, 42, 44, 45–6, 73, 83, 95–6, 105, 149–50, 166
Sudan, 31
Sudetenland, 4
Sumatra, 66, 100
Sweden, 5
Switzerland, 5
'Sword' Beach, 128
Syria, 34

Tallinn, 54
Tanks, 2, 12, 15, 30, 34, 35, 36, 37, 48, 49, 50, 53, 56, 57, 58, 64, 68, 89, 91, 92, 96, 97–8,

116–17, 118, 120, 121, 125, 129, 133, 135,
138, 140, 141–2, 143, 152, 161, 164, 172,
174, 181, 189
Taranto, 32, 186
Tedder, AM Arthur, 127
Tehran, 118, 183
Thailand, 65, 67, 153
Third Reich *see* Germany
Tirpitz, ADM, 1
Tirpitz, battleship, 43, 44, 58
Tito, Mshl, 116, 122–3
Tobruk, 35, 36, 181, 188
Tokyo, 76, 155, 191
Torpedo boat PT-109, 76
Trent Park, 131
Tripoli *see* Libya
Truman, President Harry S., 158, 178, 184, 191
Tunisia, 98, 100, 101, 116, 119, 189
    Kasserine Pass, 100
Turing, Alan, 41
Twin Axis policy, 71

U-boat, 6, 9, 35, 39–41, 42, 44–6, 58, 83,
    103–105, 185, 187, 188, 189
Ukraine, 49, 52, 89
'Ultra' intelligence, 41, 96–7, 116
    see also Bletchley Park; Enigma machine
United Kingdom, 5, 15, 24, 45, 47, 103, 122,
    177, 179
    see also Britain
United Nations, 103, 119, 184
United States (US/USA), 1, 7, 18, 29, 45,
    61, 62, 63–4, 71–3, 76, 103, 149, 156, 158,
    175, 177
    Air Force, 62, 64, 70, 71, 128, 134, 138,
        162, 163, 190, 191
    Army, 100, 129–30, 136
        82nd Airborne Division, 138
        101st Airborne Division, 138, 142
        Fifth Army, 107, 108, 109, 173
        Ninth Army, 174
        Rangers, 90, 135
        Third Army, 128, 134, 140, 143
        Twelfth Army Group, 136
        VI Corps, 111
    Army Air Force, 70, 84
    Lend-Lease, 18, 116
    Marines, 73–4, 75, 149–50, 155, 157

Navy, 62, 63, 75, 149, 154, 187
    Pacific Fleet, 62, 151
Ushijima, Lt Gen Mitsuru, 157–8
'Utah' Beach, 128

V-1 flying bomb, 132–3, 190
V-2 rocket, 133, 190
Valiant, HMS, 35, 109, 187
Valkyrie, 132
Versailles Treaty, 1, 3
Vian, Capt (later ADM), 10
Vichy France/government *see* France
Victoria, Queen, 1
Victoria Cross (VC), 11, 43, 86, 147, 148
Volga River, 91, 92

Waffen-SS *see* Germany
Walcheren Island, 137
Walker, Capt 'Johnnie', 104
Wallenberg, Raoul, 164–5
War Cabinet, British, 12, 13, 14, 33
Warsaw, 84, 121, 166
    uprising, 80, 121, 190
Warspite, HMS, 109
Washington, USA, 36–7, 63, 64, 65, 70, 71,
    98, 101, 170, 181, 182
Wavell, Gen/FM, 31, 33, 34, 70, 186, 187
Wehrmacht, 5, 34, 48, 51, 52, 53, 58–9, 89,
    109, 112, 118, 121, 122, 123, 161, 162,
    168–9, 170
Whitehall, 45
Wilhelm Gustloff, cruise liner, 166
William II (Wilhelm), Kaiser, 1
Wingate, Brig Orde, 77, 146, 153
Winton, Sir Nicholas, 165
Wolfpack tactics *see* U-boat
Women's Land Army *see* Britain, Home Front

Yalta, 167, 184
Yamamoto, ADM Isoroku, 71, 73, 76
Yamato, battleship, 157, 191
Yorktown, USS, 71, 72, 73
Yugoslavia, 32–3, 116, 122, 186

Zero fighters, 64, 72, 76, 150
Zhukov, Mar, 54, 55, 91, 92, 115, 116–17,
    118, 167, 171, 174